# Thirty-Five Logs on the Fire

## The Story of the 1984 McLeansboro Foxes' Undefeated Season

# Jeffrey Morris

# WORDS MATTER
## P U B L I S H I N G
### O U R  W O R D S  C H A N G E  T H E  W O R L D

Words Matter Publishing
P.O. Box 1190
Decatur, IL 62525
www.wordsmatterpublishing.com

ISBN: 978-1-958000-72-4
Library of Congress Catalog Card Number: 2023942018

"There is an old saying that epitomized the 1984 Foxes...
Never underestimate the Heart of a Champion...
Every player on this team was a champion." - David Lee
Head Coach 1984 McLeansboro Foxes

# Acknowledgments

For my mom and stepdad, Becky and John Prince, my dad, Steve Morris, and my stepmom, Ann Morris...Thank you for all you did for me and the sacrifices you made when I was a kid so that I could be part of such a great season. I love you all dearly.

I want to thank not only my family, but also my in-laws, Willie and Carolyn Grubb, my kid's mom, Kerri (Grubb) Tharp, and too many others to name. I would not be alive today without all of your love and support through some dark times. Thank you for always being there and helping me.

Finally, thanks to all my teammates, coaches, managers, cheerleaders, fans, and opposing players for their contributions. This book would not have been nearly as interesting without all of them taking time to respond to all my phone calls and emails.

# *Dedication*

This book is dedicated to all the kids like me who spent time playing basketball by themselves dreaming of playing for a state basketball championship.

# Foreword

The first time I thought about putting this book together was about seven years ago. Don Hill, the sportswriter for the *Times-Leader* during the eighties, had an album with lots of original pictures from the 1983-84 season. Don let me borrow them. As I went through them, I thought that people from Hamilton County would love to see these in book form. However, I could never come up with a format I liked.

Then, in November 2022, Darin Lee told me about a book Matt Wynn from Benton had written about Benton basketball coach, Rich Herrin. I bought Matt's book, *Rich Herrin: A Head Coach Ahead of His Time* and when I started reading it, I immediately thought, this is it. This is the format I need to use for a book about the 83-84 season.

I contacted Matt and asked him about the process for writing his book. Matt was so helpful. He encouraged me to use his format and even said he would help me get in touch with former Benton players to talk to about our matchups with the Rangers.

Matt also gave me some advice about putting together this book. One thing he suggested was about writing the Foreword. Matt told me that he had read a lot of history books by an author named David Mc-Cullough and McCullough's suggestion was to write the foreword by telling my connection to the subject.

I thought that would be easy. I mean, I was on the team and there for almost every moment that happened from the summer of 1983 through the seniors graduating in May 1984. As I began to think about this part of the book, it became clear that my 'connection' with the story of the '84 State Champs was bigger than just our team.

My connection was and is with the game of basketball itself. I love basketball. And when I say love, I don't mean like someone loves their favorite food or band or first car. I mean I had an obsession with basketball that was not always healthy. I ate, drank, and slept basketball from the time I was seven years old until I was well into my late twenties or even early thirties.

I was born in McLeansboro on June 29, 1967. Like a lot of kids in rural Illinois, I grew up loving the game. My parents were very young when they had me, and we were fairly strapped for money. I always had clothes and food and a home, but it was tough growing up. My parents divorced when I was six and it got even tougher. My dad was putting himself through college and my mom was raising me on her own.

My dad got his first teaching job at Eldorado High School in the summer of 1974. He was hired by the EHS athletic director, Al 'Boz' Adams, to coach freshman football in the fall, freshman basketball in the winter, and track in the spring. My mom worked odd jobs and we even lived with my grandparents off and on when I was a kid. We were scraping to get by, but I was happy.

My mom married my stepdad, John Prince, a year later and we lived in a trailer on the north side of McLeansboro. John worked for the City of McLeansboro and made about $100/week. When I was in third grade, the band teacher had all of us come to try out instruments. Mr. Prince said I was perfect for the trombone (which I suspect he said to every kid about some instrument seeing as how he needed kids in band to have a job). My mom and John sat me down and told me if I wanted to play in the band I could, but I had to stick with it if they were going to buy me an instrument. I knew what they really meant was it would be a struggle for us to pay for me to be in band, but they would find a way. I thought about it, and I knew that what I wanted to do was play ball…. and that was the end of my music career.

Dad's first year at Eldorado High School I was introduced to basketball and fell in love. Being around guys like Barry and Dennis Smith,

Mike Duff, Eddie Lane, Kevin Kingston, and others was Heaven for me. I loved being at EHS from 74-77 and loved the guys on those teams.

From that time until I stopped coaching in 1995, I was involved in basketball in some way. I watched every NCAA Final Four and tourney game. Every NBA game that I could find on television and the NBA Finals. If I could not watch the games, I would listen to the radio. I remember listening to the 1978 NBA Finals when the Washington Bullets beat the Seattle Supersonics in seven games. Dad was playing fastpitch softball for the Pinckneyville Celtics and I was sitting in our car listening to the NBA Finals during his game.

I can still name entire starting lineups for teams like the 1979 De-Paul Blue Demons and 1977 Philadelphia 76ers. I also watched every Illinois high school State Tourney from 1975-1983 and even some of the Indiana State Finals during that time. When March hits and the postseason tourneys start, you hear the term 'March Madness' said over and over.

Many people don't know that the term 'March Madness' originated in Illinois. In 1939, Henry Porter was an employee at the Illinois High School Association (IHSA) in Peoria, Illinois. Mr. Porter wrote a letter about the state tournament series that was put into the IHSA's official publication, and it was titled 'March Madness.' I wanted to play at the Assembly Hall in Champaign and be part of March Madness more than anything.

One of my first memories of my coach at MHS, David Lee, was his first year as the head coach at McLeansboro. Eldorado was undefeated and ranked number one in Class A all year in Illinois. McLeansboro was pretty good his first year but got blasted by Eldorado a couple of times. However, in Coach Lee's second year, McLeansboro beat Eldorado twice in the regular season and lost to Eldorado in the sectional finals.

Eventually, my dad left Eldorado and moved to Woodlawn (IL) high school. Dad began officiating boys' basketball in the winter and now, instead of going with dad to games at Eldorado, I was going with him wherever he was officiating. Friday night I was watching Craig Bardo and the Carbondale Terriers play Ray Blakemore and the Murphysboro Red Devils. Saturday I would get to see the Nashville Hornets and the

Pinckneyville Panthers. I knew all of the players and coaches across Southern Illinois and my favorite time of year was the state tournament.

In 1978 I watched Nashville high school and Bob Bogle win the state title by beating the Havana Ducks and I knew that I wanted to play in Champaign when I was in high school.

I did not become a fan of the McLeansboro Foxes until I moved into junior high and played for Curt Reed, Sr. If you have never met Coach Reed, you just need to know his nickname is 'Crazy Horse' and it fits. Nobody could get you more fired up to play a basketball game than Curt.

My first time going to a Foxes' game and feeling like I wanted to play for Coach Lee was during the 1980-81 season. That was Coach Lee's best team up to that point in his time at MHS. They finished the season 24-5 with a disappointing loss in the regional finals to West Frankfort. However, I remember watching Brad Lee, Darin Lee, and the rest of the 80-81 team play and I knew I wanted to play for the Foxes.

Like lots of kids in the rural Midwest, I spent hours and hours playing basketball. Outside on the playground and in the gym at Woodlawn high school. I was lucky to have a dad who had a key to the gym, and I was there all the time. I would be at WHS all day and even late in the night on the weekends and summer. I even set up a television in the gym so I could watch the NCAA tournament games and shoot at the same time.

I won't say that I loved the game or worked harder at it than anyone else. Lots of guys like me played a lot of basketball. The difference between me and a lot of others was just luck. I was lucky to be at MHS and be a Fox at the right time. Any of a number of guys I played against in high school could have done what I did for the 83-84 team. Guys like Stacy Woolsey from Carmi, Glenn Hall from NCOE, Brad Hummert, Mark Etter, Ron Schadegg from Breese Mater Dei, and, Matt Wynn from Benton could have easily taken my place and made our team even better.

One of my favorite authors is Malcolm Gladwell author of 'Outliers.' In the book, he talks about the myth of people who work the hardest being the most successful. What he found in his research is that most of the time successful people are just lucky and take advantage of that luck. For example, Bill Gates and all the other tech billionaires were not smarter and did not work harder than everyone else. They just happened to be born at the right time in the 1950s. Don't get me wrong, all those guys and gals were smart and worked hard, but not at a level that made them smarter or harder working than lots of other people.

Even Bill Gates said he was just lucky (Gladwell, 2008). Bill Gates attended a small, private high school in the late 1960s and one year the Mother's Club bought a computer (Galdwell, 2008). Bill and his pals latched on to that thing and they spent every spare moment learning how to use it and what it could do. Steve Joy, the founder of Sun Microsystems, was like Bill Gates. Joy went to college in the early 70s to study biology but just happened to attend the University of Michigan at a time when they had one of the first computer labs in the nation (Gladwell, 2008). He happened on to that lab by accident and the rest was history (Gladwell, 2008). Gates and Joy both were just lucky and took advantage of their good fortune, but they did not do it alone (Gladwell, 2008).

I was the same way. I was not a great player. I was not super athletic, but I was lucky, and I was willing to do whatever we needed to win. I took advantage of having access to a gym at Woodlawn high school whenever I wanted. When my friends were going out and doing other stuff on Friday night, I was at the gym till 11:00 p.m. I did not care about scoring or my name getting in the paper. I just wanted to play basketball and compete. I was 'every kid.' By that I mean I was just a typical kid from Southern Illinois who happened to be on a team with great teammates and coaches. I was just lucky to be part of the ride.

When people bring up the 83-84 season, one of the questions I get is, 'What made you guys so great?' Well, I can talk about that for hours, but it was just a few simple things. First, we were great in part because we did not think we were great. We knew we had to be ready to play against most of the teams on our schedule to be able to have a chance to win.

Second, we had great chemistry. Each of us knew our roles and were all unselfish enough to not worry about individual stats. Never once in all my time playing in High School did I ever witness any dissension or jealousy among our players.

Finally, we had great coaches and took advantage of having such great coaches. What I mean is that it does no good to have great coaches if the players are not 'coachable' and vice versa. It was a 'perfect storm' of really good coaches and really good players who did what the coaches wanted us to do.

I wish that every player like me could have experienced what I did in the 1983-84 season because my connection is with them. I hope this book gives you an idea of what it was like. Enjoy.

# Contents

# Table of Contents

"It is amazing what can be accomplished if
you do not care who gets the credit."

*-President Harry S. Truman*

# 1

# The Day It Started.... February 17, 1982

If there was ever a time to rob a bank in the history of McLeansboro, Illinois, it was the weekend of March 17, 1984. An illness had been ravaging the community since early December 1983 and had turned McLeansboro into a ghost town. Like the Dustin Hoffman movie *Outbreak*, the homes, businesses, and streets were empty. The illness was not deadly, but it was highly contagious and had been passed on to almost everyone in Hamilton County. This illness was called 'Fox Fever'. In fact, you, and others you knew at the time may have been among the thousands who were suffering from 'Fox Fever' the night the Foxes captured the Illinois State Title by beating the Mt. Pulaski Hilltoppers 57-50 to finish a perfect 35-0.

Wait, wait, wait....before we get to talking about the 83-84 season, we have to go back a bit. We have to talk about the long history of great teams and players who wore Kelly Green for the Foxes. Long before cassette tapes and "making laps around the square" and hanging out at Pat's Café and big hair and MTV.

McLeansboro high school has a long and storied history of great basketball players and teams. In the late 50s and into the mid-60s, the Foxes were a state power. This little school of about 500 students with only a couple of stoplights in the town produced some of the best basketball teams in the state of Illinois.

In 1959-60, the Foxes were led by future Chicago Bull, Jerry Sloan, as well as Curt Reed Sr, and future SIU-C Saluki David Lee. They also had a freshman on the bench named Jim Burns. Jim would lead the Foxes to a third-place finish in 1962 and go on to be one of the leading scorers at Northwestern before a brief career with the Chicago Bulls and the Dallas Chaparrals in the ABA.

In the late 60s and early 70s, the program was struggling and had several losing seasons. David Lee was hired as the head coach at McLeansboro high school before the 1975-76 season and the program began to improve each year under Coach Lee's leadership. However, I believe the key event that led to the undefeated state title season in 1983-84 happened almost two years before that season even took place. In fact, it did not even happen near McLeansboro, Illinois.

In the 1981-82 season I was a freshman at MHS. The previous year the Foxes were 24-5 and had a senior-laden team. The only player who was returning in 81-82 who had played much was David's son, Darin. The 81-82 team was not expected to do much with one senior. However, a number of the guys from the 60s had sons who were in school at that time. In addition to Darin Lee, Curt Reed, Jr was a junior, and Tracy Sturm— whose dad Tom started on the 1961-62 team that finished third in the state—was a sophomore. Darin, Curty, Tracy, sophomore Scott Cravens, and Danny Anselment—the only senior on the team—ended up being the starting five and finished the season with a record of 22-5. Although they lost in the regional to an outstanding Benton Ranger team that year, there was a lot of optimism for the 1982-83 season with only one graduating senior.

A few months before the end of the 81-82 season, something happened that started a chain of events that led to the 83-84 team coming together. The date was February 17, 1982, in Chicago, Illinois on Madison Avenue at the old Chicago Stadium....that was the day that Jerry Sloan was fired by the Chicago Bulls as head coach after less than three years.

Jerry played for the Bulls for about a decade before retiring in 1976 due to a knee injury. Jerry played for the Baltimore Bullets (now Washington Wizards) during his rookie season in 1965 and then was the first player the Chicago Bulls drafted in the 1966 expansion draft. Jerry Sloan was known as the 'Original Chicago Bull.' Jerry was beloved by the Bulls' fans, and he was the first player to have his number retired by the franchise in 1978. Jerry became an assistant to the Bulls' head coach, Dick Motta. Before the 1979-80 season, Jerry was named head coach of the Chicago Bulls.

Even though it was likely one of Jerry's toughest days, little did any of us know that that day would mean that Jerry would be moving home the following summer and bringing his family, including his son Brian, with him.

***Dr. Brian Sloan, MHS Class of '84 and 1984 Illinois Mr. Basketball:*** *After Dad was let go by the Bulls in February of 1982, he wanted to get out of Chicago. Mom had no interest in moving and did not want to move back to their hometown, McLeansboro, Illinois.*

*But Dad told us, "It is time for us to leave Chicago." We loved living in Northbrook, but I think Dad just felt like he needed to distance himself from the city and the Bulls after he was fired as the head coach. Dad was a hard worker and being fired from a job is about the worst thing that could happen to someone like him.*

***Holly (Sloan) Parrish, Brian Sloan's sister and MHS Class of '88:*** *"If my dad did not lose his job with the Bulls in 1982, we would probably have never moved to McLeansboro. My family loved Northbrook and Dad did not want to be a journeyman. The two seasons Brian played at MHS were likely the silver lining for Dad losing his job with the Bulls."*

The Sloan family bought an old house on Washington St and moved to McLeansboro after Brian had finished his sophomore year at Glenbrook North high school. Heading into the 1982-83 season there were high hopes for the Foxes to return to Champaign and a shot at a state title. That 82-83 team had a tremendous season and finished 31-4. However, Darin Lee suffered a severe ankle injury in the opening game of the state finals. Darin tried to play against Flanagan in the semifinals, but they ended up losing 39-34. If Darin had been healthy, I believe they would have beaten Flanagan and matched up well with Lawrenceville, the eventual state champs. The Foxes ended up finishing third in Class A in 1983.

Heading into the summer of 1983, there was once again a lot of optimism for the upcoming season. Brian Sloan and Tracy Sturm were returning. Stacy Sturm, Tracy's younger brother, and Brian Cross were both 6'3 going into their junior season and expected to contribute. Scott Cravens did not play basketball in his junior season, but he was going to play his senior season.

I had lived with my dad in Woodlawn, Illinois the previous year and had a good year playing varsity for the Cardinals as a sophomore. But I decided to go back to MHS for my junior year.

That summer we went to Jerry Sloan's camp in Aurora and all of us reconnected again. We played in a few tournaments and played pretty well, but there was no indication of what was about to come in the upcoming basketball season. I believe there was a sense we would be pretty good, but there were still questions about how good.

The 1965 College Division Championship game at Roberts Stadium in Evansville, IN. The Evansville Aces, led by Jerry Sloan (52), would beat the SIU Salukis, led by David Lee (20), in overtime to claim the title.

Jerry Sloan playing for the Evansville Aces vs Iowa in 1965. Jerry would lead the Aces to the College Division title in 1965 and then be drafted by the Baltimore Bullets (now Washington Wizards) in the NBA Draft. Jerry would then be selected by the expansion Chicago Bulls in the 1st round of the expansion draft the following year.

The only two former Foxes to have their numbers retired at MHS are Jerry Sloan and Jim Burns. Jerry wore #54 and Jim wore #52. Jerry was a senior in 1960 and Jim was a freshman the same year. They were also teammates on the Chicago Bulls for three games at the start of the 1967-68. So, McLeansboro High School, a small rural school of under 500 students had two future NBA players on their team at the same time in 1959-60.

Jerry Sloan diving for a loose ball against the Philadelphia 76ers when Jerry was playing for the Chicago Bulls. Jerry was known as "The Original Bull" since he was the first player drafted by the franchise in 1966. He would go on to have a great career and be the first Chicago Bull to have his number retired.

February 17, 1982..... picture from Jerry Sloan's press conference when he was fired from the Bulls. I doubt Jerry was thinking about how this would turn out for his alma mater and the community in his home town.

# 2

## The Summer of 1983

Before getting into the 1983-84 season, it is important to understand how close we were to not coming together. The 82-83 team was really good. They were likely more talented than the 83-84 team and played a tougher schedule. Brian Sloan and Tracy Sturm were returning, and Stacy Sturm and Bryan Cross had been the leading scorers for the junior varsity the previous year.

Scott Cravens had started most of the 81-82 season and played well, but he did not play as a junior. I don't know why Scott did not play, but Coach Lee has said that he was not sure if Scott would have played much varsity in the 82-83 season because that team was really deep. They had at least two guys on the bench, Scott Wilkerson and Rod Irvin, who could have started for most Class A teams in Southern Illinois.

*Don Hill, Sportswriter for the Times-Leader: One of the most important events leading up to that season was Scott Cravens coming back out for basketball as a senior. Scott did not play in 82-83 and David knew he needed another player who could help the team. David went to Dahlgren that summer and talked Scott into playing again.*

I had spent my sophomore year living with my dad in Woodlawn, Illinois, and playing for the Woodlawn Cardinals. Several people I have talked to thought I only attended school in McLeansboro during my junior and senior years, but that is not true. I was born in McLeansboro and attended every year but kindergarten (I lived in Oakland City, Indiana while my dad was a student at Oakland City College) in Hamilton County Unit #10.

My first experience playing organized basketball was on the fifth-grade team with Coach Lew Reed, the high school football coach at the time. One game we played the Beaver Creek Bombers, a small school in the Hamilton County District in the northern part of the county. I made like four twenty-foot shots in the game. Even though I am pretty sure I missed the other twenty shots I took, I had never had a feeling like that before. Hearing a ball 'swoosh' through the net without touching the rim is like listening to Mozart's Overture to *The Marriage of Figaro* for a basketball player. Coach Lew Reed was impressed, and I felt like a superstar. That was the point where I wanted to get better.

I played on the seventh-grade team as a sixth grader and by eighth grade I was one of the better players at East Side Junior High. We had a good team in my eighth-grade year and I had a good season. I was excited about going to play at MHS.

My freshman year started off a little rough. My first game was at Benton high school, and I made an ass out of myself by being really cocky and showing off. That was not going to fly with Coach Lee or my dad.

The next day at school, Coach Lee called me to his office and chewed me up, and spit me out. I was such a jerk that Rich Herrin called my dad and told him how I acted. I went to see Dad on Friday and when he got home from calling his game that night, he woke me up and chewed on me as well. Trust me, I never so much as pumped my fist during a game after that.

The rest of my freshman year went well. Stacy Sturm, Bryan Cross, Jim Melton, Tim Biggerstaff, Jim Ingram, and others were on the freshman team. I had a really good year as a freshman. In one of our first games, we played at Carmi right before Christmas break and were down one with about seven seconds left in the game. Carmi was shooting a one-and-one and I knew I had to get the ball quickly so we could get a shot. I was only about 5'7, but I grabbed Jim Ingram and told him to let me get on the inside position for the rebound. Amazingly, I got the rebound off the miss, dribbled the full length of the floor, and hit a ten-footer at the buzzer to win. I never thought it was a big deal, but it did feel good to make that shot. Once again, I fell in love with the game even more. I wanted that feeling again.

Right after the Eldorado Holiday Tournament, Coach Lee moved me up to the junior varsity team. Now, this may not seem like that big of a deal, but for me it was huge. We had a really good JV team. Kevin Kirsch, Rod Irvin, Scott Wilkerson, and Troy Lueke were all juniors and started along with Ernie Shelton. That year, our JV team could have competed with a lot of teams in Southern Illinois.

My first game was against Z-R. Gary Burzynski, our junior varsity coach, put me in midway through the first quarter. I was kind of shell-shocked because there were already so many people at the game. I ended up making all six shots I took and scoring twelve points. Again, my confidence level was getting higher. Not cocky or arrogant, but I just felt good about how I was playing.

My schedule for the rest of the season was pretty much like this five days a week:

8:00 a.m.     Get to school.

3:00 p.m.     Practice with either the freshman team or the JV/Varsity.

5:00 p.m.     Go to the arcade across the street from MHS, get a bite to eat, play video games, and do my homework.

6:00 p.m.     Play in either a freshman or JV game.

10:00 p.m. (or later) Get home.

For most teenagers, this likely sounds horrible. Not for kids like me. If there was a Heaven, as far as I was concerned, this was it.

I played well with the JV team, and we had a good season on the freshman team. The varsity lost to the Benton Rangers in the Regional Final that year. We had a very young, but talented team that surprised a lot of people by finishing 22-5.

At that time, Murphysboro hosted a sophomore tournament every year after the regular season was over. The first Saturday after the regional, we went to Murphysboro high school to take on the Pinckneyville Panthers' sophomores. I was excited to play at Murphy because I had watched guys like Ray Blackemore, and the Kellum brothers play a few years before. I also knew their coach at the time, DeWayne Kelly, because he played a lot of fastpitch softball against my dad. Coach Kelly also played for Coach Lee when David was at Carbondale High School in the early 70s.

We were warming up for the game and I was ready to play.

At that point, I heard someone on our team, after they looked at the Panthers, say, "We are gonna get killed."

I did not say a word, but I thought, not if I have anything to do with it! I had maybe the best game I ever played in High School by scoring about thirty points. Tony Rubenacker, Ernie Shelton, Heath Lasswell, Stacy Sturm, and Bryan Cross all played well, and we won by about ten points.

Our next game was against the Benton Rangers, and they had a really good group of sophomores. Darren Carlisle, Jay Bradshaw, and Troy Hewlitt were good players. Carbondale played Murphysboro before us, and they were really good. Their best player was Glenn Martin, who would go on to play at Drake University. Glenn was lightning quick, a great jumper, and had played some varsity for the Terriers that year. I watched the game and thought, if we beat Benton, I am gonna have to guard him. At the time, I was probably too dumb to realize how he was going to kill me.

We played Benton tough but lost in a fairly close game. We ended the season by losing to Murphysboro in the third-place game of the tournament.

As the school year ended, I began to think about living with my dad in Woodlawn. My parents divorced when I was six and, although I saw Dad a lot, I had never lived with him. I talked to my mom and told her I wanted to move. It was a tough decision for all of us, but I was excited. Woodlawn was like a second home to me, and I had many friends there.

I spent my sophomore year at Woodlawn and had a great year. I started varsity most of the year and we had a really fun team. We finished 22-5 and were led by Jerry Boldt, one of the all-time leading scorers in the history of Illinois High School basketball. Our team was very small, but we were talented and ran like crazy. Jerry, Rick Gaebe, Scott Langa, Scott Owens, and the late Brian Mitchell were a lot of fun to play with at WHS.

Our season ended in the regional with a loss to Okawville 86-73. Jerry scored thirty-six points, but we had no answer for 6'6 Paul Jansen, who scored forty-two himself. After the game, we were pretty down and sitting in the locker room when the door opens, and in walks Okawville's coach, Dave Luechtefeld.

Coach Luechtefeld is a very stoic and intimidating man. He stands about 6'7 and always seemed very cool and calm. He came in and said something like, "In over twenty years of coaching, I have never gone to an opponent's locker room after a game, but I have to tell you that no team has ever battled us as hard as you guys did tonight. You all should be proud of yourselves." Okawville would go on to lose to the McLeansboro Foxes in the 1983 super-sectional.

I was planning to finish my High School years at Woodlawn, but after the year ended my dad asked me about going back to McLeansboro. He told me it was my decision, and he would support whatever I wanted to do. I was really torn. I had played well, and we were going to be really good the next year at WHS. I spent a few days thinking about what to do and decided it was just too good an opportunity to pass up playing with Brian and the rest of the Foxes.

I spent the summer back and forth between playing basketball with the Foxes and playing summer baseball in Woodlawn. I went to the Sloan, Lee, Reed camp and also went to Jerry Sloan's camp in Aurora with most of the rest of our team. We also played in a couple of summer tournaments against other teams from Southern Illinois.

We did not have Scott Cravens with us, so we really had no idea how good we could be. We played all right all summer. The one thing that stands out was when we played Cairo at Rend Lake College that summer. Cairo beat us by about fifteen points and made it look pretty easy. We had some time between games and were all sitting outside with

Coach Lee. David said something very prophetic when he told us, "Forget about this loss to Cairo. We will kick their asses during the season because we will have Cravens and you will be better prepared to face them next time." He could not have been more right. By August, I had moved back to my mom's and was ready to start school.

*David Lee: During the summer of 1983 I began to think about the 83-84 basketball season. Since we had the experience of going to State and with the players that we had returning, I thought we could be really good. As the season began, I could see that we had the players to be very competitive.*

*Holly Sloan: I thought it would be really hard to top the season before. I didn't know any of the new players (Jeff Morris, Stacy Sturm, Bryan Cross). I mean, I knew them but had no idea what they would bring to the remaining players. Also, at the time, we didn't know that Scott Cravens would be returning.*

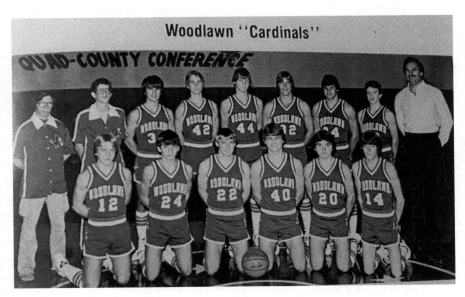

The 1982-83 Woodlawn Cardinals…. I attended Woodlawn my sophomore year and we had a great season. We finished 22-5 and won the Quad County Conference. Choosing to leave WHS and go back to McLeansboro was one of the hardest decisions of my young life. I loved playing at Woodlawn with these guys.

# 3

🏀

# *Preseason*

We spent the fall of 1983 doing conditioning with Curt Reed. Coach Reed had been the eighth-grade coach at East Side Jr. High for the previous decade. Many of the guys on the team had played for Coach Reed at East Side and he had just been named the junior varsity coach prior to the 1983-84 school year.

Most of the players on the team were not in a fall sport, so we spent the fall lifting and running every day during our last hour of PE class. Monday through Friday, we would spend the last hour of PE lifting weights and then conditioning with Coach Reed. It was not fun, but we knew we needed to be in shape for the start of the season in November. I remember that Brian Sloan set the tone for us. Every Friday we ran a mile at the track and every Friday Brian finished first. Brian was not only our best player, but he was also our hardest worker.

***Brian Sloan:*** *I did not do anything special to get better for my senior year. I think the main reason I was better as a senior was that I just got a little bit stronger and matured both physically and mentally between my junior and senior year.*

One interesting thing about preseason was that Coach Lee was not involved with us much. I don't know if he did that purposely, but Coach

Reed did all of the conditioning with us in the fall. Looking back, I think that was a good decision by Coach Lee because he was going to be on us all season and we might have gotten tired of hearing his voice if he had added the entire fall to that season.

During that time, Brian Sloan and I became really good friends. Brian had played football his junior year but had decided not to play as a senior. I was lucky to be able to spend a lot of time with Brian and his family. Brian was getting recruited by several Division 1 schools in the Midwest.

Brian talked about wanting to pick a school before the season so that he could enjoy his senior year. I remember Brian visited Purdue and Indiana University that fall and would come back and tell me about his recruitment. I loved hearing about his trips and meeting Coach Keady and Coach Knight. I was a huge IU fan, so I hoped he would choose IU.

Jim Crews was the top assistant at IU that year and came to MHS to talk to Brian that fall. I remembered watching Coach Crews when he played on the 1976 IU team that went undefeated and won the National Title against Michigan. I am fairly certain I was the only player, besides Brian, who had any idea who Coach Crews was.

Brian ended up choosing to go to IU after he graduated from MHS. All of us were happy for Brian and proud that he had chosen to go play at IU for Coach Knight. I also knew that Brian was happy to have that process over and get ready for the upcoming season.

**Don Lewis, Class of '86/Team Manager:** *I was cleaning the basketballs in the coach's office when the phone rang, I answered, "Hello, coach's office."*

*The voice on the other line said, "Hello, this is Bobby Knight. May I speak to Coach Lee?"*

*I then had to run back to the school to find Coach Lee. I couldn't find him, so I had other staff call for him over the intercom. We both ran over to the coach's office. Coach Lee then had me run back over to his office on the other side of the gym to grab his tape recorder.*

**Bryan Cross, Foxes' sixth Man:** *I thought we would have a very good team. The '83 team finished third the year before and, with Brian and Tracy back, there was a lot of optimism about the '84 season. That excitement only grew when I heard Scott Cravens was coming back out. With you and Stacy, there were a lot of good players in place for a great season.*

**Heath Lasswell, Foxes' Senior Reserve:** *I felt like we had the essentials for a successful team. With Tracy and Brian back from the year before; plus, speed, rebounding, and outside shooting. All of these qualities were the makings of a good team. Then, we just needed to be led in the right direction.*

## Close friends

David Lee, Jerry Sloan and Curt Reed Sr. (from left) developed an abiding friendship when they played together at McLeansboro. After each went on to college ball and Sloan to the pro ranks, they were reunited last year. Sloan and Reed currently assist Lee at practice. (Courier photo by Tom Gundy)

Coach Lee, Jerry Sloan, and Curt Reed all played together at MHS in the late 50s and early 60s. They came back and their son's Darin Lee, Brian Sloan, and Curt Reed Jr played together on the 82-83 Foxes' team that finished 3rd in the Class A State Tournament.

# 4

## *Practice Starts*

We had our first practice on a cold, Monday morning in early November. We always practiced twice a day for the first two weeks of the season. Morning practices were from 7-8 a.m. Coach Lee would bring us donuts and orange juice so that we had something for breakfast before school. We all showered, went to class, and then we would practice for about three hours or so after school. Preseason practice was about three weeks until we opened the season.

I am fairly certain all of us knew we had a chance to be pretty good for the upcoming season. We never talked about expectations, going undefeated, or winning the state title. I don't think any of us had any idea what was about to happen. The year before McLeansboro had finished third in Class A with a 31-4 record. However, that team lost a lot of talent.

Darin Lee, Curtie Reed, Kevin Kirsch, Rod Irvin, and Scott Wilkerson had all graduated. Brian Sloan and Tracy Sturm were returning starters. Brian led the team in scoring and rebounding in 82-83 and Tracy averaged in double figures. Scott Cravens was coming back to play his senior year after sitting out as a junior. Ernie Shelton also looked like he might play some as a senior. Stacy Sturm and Bryan Cross had played junior varsity the previous year and were expected to compete for starting positions. I had moved back from Woodlawn for my junior year and thought I might be able to play a little as well.

**Don Hill:** *I knew we were going to be good, but not sure how good. We had some experience coming back with Tracy and Sloan. Cravens was coming back out. David Lee had also learned a lot the previous year about how to prepare for the post-season and Curt Reed was the new JV coach. Things looked very promising for a great season.*

Every year before the first game, Coach Lee would give the players a folder with stories about the previous season and also what we wanted to accomplish during the upcoming season. The 1983-84 folder had reminders from the previous season and the success that team had during the year. I believe Coach Lee just wanted to plant the seed that we wanted to get back to the state tourney without actually saying it.

I do remember that we always had the same goals each year when the season started:

1. Win the Eldorado Holiday Tourney.
2. Win the Benton Invitational Tourney.
3. Win the Regional.
4. Have more class than any team in Southern Illinois.

I am certain that all of us knew we had higher goals than these four.

**Scott Cravens:** *Clearly there was an expectation of having a great team. But even with great talent, teamwork, and coaching, it doesn't always end in an undefeated season. The players came into the season with everything you need for a great team— speed, size, rebounding, strong defense, shooting, ball handling, and a strong desire to win.*

**Heath Lasswell:** *One of the funny memories I have was during practices. Coach Lee would have some of us players use wiffle ball bats to contest Brian when he was working on shooting in the post. I thought it was funny at the time, but as I look back now it was a good strategy to help Brian get better. However, when the coaches were not looking, things would get a little dicey with those bats. We were lucky we did not get tossed out of practice.*

On the second Sunday of pre-season, we had a scrimmage against former players and other guys from the community who could still play. Former players like Brad Lee, Bryan "Soup" Campbell, Kevin Kirsch, and others would come in to play against us. However, Jerry Sloan also played against us.

If you knew Jerry Sloan, then you know that when he played, he was the most physical basketball player any of us had ever competed against. Jerry was legendary in the NBA for going up against guys like Wilt Chamberlain and Bill Russell. I think Jerry might have given up his firstborn child to get a rebound.

Jerry was in his early forties and, even though he had a bad knee and could not straighten one of his arms, he could still dominate a bunch of young kids. The previous year, Jerry had a jump ball against Darin Lee. Darin made the mistake of putting his arm out to prevent Jerry from winning the tip. Jerry went right through Darin and broke Darin's wrist. Darin had to sit out the first few games of the season.

Jerry always guarded Brian and I do remember that Jerry beat Brian for the better part of two hours. If Brian ever needed a reminder of who the best player was in the Sloan family, he got it on that day. I also remember taking a charge on Jerry and when he ran over me, I thought for a brief second about Darin getting hurt. I remember thinking Jerry had put his forearm through my sternum and into my spine. But I jumped up and was just a little worse for wear. In the end, we made it through the pre-season practices and were ready to open the season.

One of the constants of our season was Jerry Sloan being on the peripheral with our team. I knew that Jerry helped Coach Lee and his staff a great deal in preparation, scouting, and game-planning, but Jerry never once was part of any of our video sessions or anything else we did to prepare for a game.

During most practices, Jerry was seated on the south side of the MHS gym in the very top row of the bleachers. He watched practice and never said a word. Jerry ran one of our practices with Coach Smith-peters, our freshman coach, on a day when Coach Lee and Coach Reed had to be at staff training. I was at the Sloan's house a lot during the season and the only time Jerry ever said anything to me about our team or the season was when he told me I played well against DuQuoin.

Jerry Sloan was one of the most humble and grounded men I have ever met, and you will likely notice that even though he was a great NBA player and a Hall of Fame NBA Coach, he is not mentioned a lot in this book. I imagine that is the way Jerry would have wanted it. Jerry, who passed away on May 22, 2020, was an important part of our success in the 1983-84 season, but he never once acknowledged how much he helped us that year. Jerry had many great experiences playing and coaching in the NBA, but I always wondered if he did not rank watching his son win a state title and be named Illinois Mr. Basketball up there with any of those memories.

*David Lee: Throughout the season Jerry Sloan went with me to scout a team and helped to break down the film. Jerry always said, "Every team has its weaknesses." However, Jerry never interfered with coaching. He often told anyone that made comments about the coaching that his son and the team had ONE coach and he was on the bench.*

*Brian Sloan: Dad never said much about how I played in High School. All he wanted me to do was compete hard every game and be a good teammate. Mom was the one who would get on me if I did not play as hard or as well as she thought I should have played. I think Dad just enjoyed being able to watch our team play for the two years I was at MHS and the fact that we finished third in 1983 and then won it all in 1984 made it that much sweeter for all of us.*

# 5

# The Season Opens
## Game 1: Foxes 54 Vienna Eagles 29
## Foxes 1-0

On Friday, December 1, 1983, we opened the season against the Vienna Eagles. The game was really never in doubt. We led 30-16 at the half and by the fourth quarter, Coach Lee had emptied the bench to get everyone in the game. Brian Sloan led us with twenty points, twenty rebounds, and five blocks, Tracy Sturm had ten points and nine rebounds and Stacy chipped in with ten points and eight boards.

It was a good win for us to start the season, but the thing I remember most was warming up before the game and looking up in the stands. On the top row of the bleachers, I saw Coach Rich Herrin and several Benton Rangers players with their shaved heads. Randy House, Bruce Baker, and a few others were with Coach Herrin to watch us play. It was a reminder that we had a huge game coming up the following Sunday at SIU Arena in Carbondale.

Another interesting thing about this game was the coach at Vienna at that time was Max Hook. In 1989, Darin Lee was hired as the head coach at Vienna and Max was his assistant for two seasons. In 1991, Darin left to become the head coach at Nashville (IL) High School, and I was hired to replace Darin as the head coach at VHS. Max was my assistant for four seasons, and I coached his son, Lucas, for three years. Max has remained friends with Darin and me for many years.

***Nicole VanZant, Senior Cheerleader:*** *I do remember the bus rides to and from the games... especially going to the games. You could hear a pin drop. It wasn't a bunch of High School kids, laughing and cutting up and having fun on the way to a game. It was serious business, but we all understood it and never minded it.*

*I can remember feeling very confident as a cheerleader when we would go to do our hello cheer to the other squad. As we would wish them the best of luck, I can remember thinking, you're gonna need it. I also remember my dad, MHS principal Ernie VanZant, was relieved that all the players were good kids and students. He knew if he had to suspend one of you guys, he would have likely been run out of town.*

Stacy Sturm scores in our season opener against the Vienna Eagles.

# 6

## Foxes vs Benton Rangers at the Tip-Off Classic at SIU Arena
## Game 2: Foxes 61 Benton Rangers 55
## Foxes 2-0

In the 1970s and 80s, SIU Arena was the mecca of Southern Illinois basketball. The Arena hosted the Class A and AA Super-sectional every year, with the winner going to the state tournament. I had been to lots of games at SIUC, but walking into SIU Arena for the first time as a player was special for me. I saw many great High School games there.

One of the first times I had heard about SIU Arena was in the winter of 1977. I went to stay with my dad on a Friday and he handed me an SIU Saluki program and said, "Jeff, I saw the greatest college player I have ever seen this week...this guy from Indiana State named Larry Bird." I kept that program and memorized it from cover to cover. A year later, Bird and ISU would lose to Magic Johnson and the Michigan St. Spartans in the NCAA title game.

Now, it is very common for High School basketball teams in this day and age to play in 'Shootouts' or 'Jamboree' type events. Typically, this means that a school or college will host a day of games with teams from all over a state or even the nation. It is a great way for fans to see a number of teams and players at one event.

These types of basketball events were just starting to take off in the early 80s. Southern Illinois University at Carbondale had started hosting a 'Tip Off Classic' and inviting some of the top teams in Southern Illinois to participate. On December 4, 1983, SIU hosted a three-game tip-off with the following matchups:

Game 1:    Mounds Meridian Bobcats vs Cairo Pilots
- The two schools were bitter rivals from Pulaski County in deep, Southern Illinois and had some great players like JJ Strickland from Meridian and Shawn Box from Cairo.

Game 2:    Benton Rangers vs McLeansboro Foxes

Game 3:    Carbondale Terriers vs Belleville Althoff
- Carbondale was absolutely loaded with Glenn Martin (Drake University), Joe Hamilton, Doug Altecruse, Ronnie Tate, and Stephen Bardo (who played for the Illinois Illini).

There was a lot of hype heading into this game. Benton and McLeansboro had always been rivals since Benton is about twenty miles west of McLeansboro in neighboring Franklin County. Benton and McLeansboro both had a long history of talented players like former Rangers Doug Collins (yes, that Doug Collins), Rich Yunkus, Bill Smith, Rob Dunbar, and Danny Johnson, and former Foxes like Jerry Sloan, Curt Reed, David Lee, Jim and John Burns, and Carl Mauck (who played for about a decade in the NFL).

Benton had one of the best basketball programs in the state and was ranked among the top AA teams, even though they were one of the smaller AA schools. In fact, Benton had switched between class A and AA multiple times in the early 80s.

The rivalry with Benton had been pretty one-sided during the 1970s up to 1982. Coach Herrin always had a good team with great players. In the 1981-82 season, Benton beat us twice, but we were competitive with them. In 1982-83, the Rangers won the season opener, but the Foxes got their revenge in the final game of the BIT by beating the Rangers 66-63 in overtime. It would be the first of several great games from 1983-1985.

This year's game between Benton and McLeansboro was much like the previous season in that both teams had plenty of talent and size as well. Benton had five players who would go on to play college basketball. Bruce Baker was 6'7 and one of the best players in the state. Bruce was All-State in 1982-83 and would go on to play at the University of Alabama at Birmingham. He was not a great athlete, but he was very crafty and could score inside and out. Kai Nurnberger was a 6' exchange student from Germany and would go on to play at SIUC. Kai was a terrific player who scored over 1000 points at SIUC and even played on the German Olympic team in 1992 with Detlef Shrempf and faced the Dream Team. Benton also had Darren Carlisle (6'3 guard), Randy House (6'5 forward), and Marion (IL) high school transfer Jay Schaefer (6'7 center), all of whom would go on to play at SIUC for Rich Herrin.

The Foxes also had five players who would go on to play in college. Brian Sloan played at Indiana University. Tracy and Stacy Sturm both played at Rend Lake CC and then at Lambuth College (TN). Bryan Cross ended his playing career at RLC, and I also went to RLC and then played at the University of Wisconsin-Superior.

**Ron Smith, Benton Rangers' Asst. Coach:** *Brian Sloan and Bruce Baker were two of the premier big men in the Southern Illinois that year. Two of the best in the state. Both were outstanding players, played so hard, and were very likable and enjoyable to be around both on and off the court.*

*The supporting cast around both those guys on both teams had similar qualities. They were all great competitors in their own right. Each of their skill sets and willingness to accept their roles that would best serve their team was sometimes unnoticed by fans. As a coach, I know how important it is for each player to adjust and find out how they can best help their team win.*

*One of my favorite quotes is 'Don't strive to be the BEST PLAYER on the TEAM... Strive to be the BEST PLAYER for the TEAM.'*

*Benton and McLeansboro had about twenty to thirty guys players dressed for those two games who epitomized that idea.*

We all knew that this was going to be a tough game and we would have to play well to have a chance to win. Going into the game I think we had a couple of advantages. First, some of Benton's players had played football that year for the first time. Normally, that would not have impacted the basketball season, but Benton always played West Frankfort on Thanksgiving Day. That meant that they could not practice with their full team until after that game was played. This meant we had about a two-week head start leading into the game. Second, Kai Nurnberger and Jay Schaefer were new to Benton, so without practice time with Baker, House, etc. it would mean they might not have great chemistry for their first game.

The game was very close throughout. We led at the end of the first quarter 14-10 and led at the half by a score of 34-29. Brian was dominant the entire first half. We ran a play called Kansas St. over and over. The play called for me to enter the ball to Brian at the free throw line and for us to clear out the side for him. Brian torched the Rangers for thirty points and eleven rebounds in the game. That was a really tough matchup for Jay Schaefer in his first start as a sophomore in High School.

**Ernie Shelton, MHS Class of 84, Guard:** *I can remember in practice catching an elbow from Brian Sloan right under my nose and thinking why am I in the paint trying to get a rebound? Purely unintentional but I couldn't imagine the pain he inflicted on so many in the paint.*

In the third quarter, Brian picked up his fourth foul. Benton led 43-39 with about two minutes to go and Bryan Cross had replaced Brian. We ran a continuity offense that a lot of teams used called 'The Flex'. Jerry Sloan showed it to Coach Lee when he came back from Chicago the previous year. We had used 'Flex' the previous year when I played at Woodlawn High School.

Lots of teams ran it to score, but we used it as a delay game sometimes. We ran 'Flex', or 'Spot' as we called it, for the last two minutes of the quarter. Benton's fans cheered thinking they were playing great defense. We had one plan…hold the ball for the rest of the quarter and get an open jumper for Bryan Cross. We ran the clock down and Cross hit an elbow jumper with about two seconds left in the quarter to draw us within two points at 43-41.

We ended up outscoring Benton 20-12 in the final frame. The final score was 61-55. Brian was terrific. He was clearly the best player on the floor that game. Brian was such an unselfish player and a great leader. He could have scored thirty-plus points every game, but he was a better passer, defender, and rebounder. Brian always seemed to have his best games when we needed them from him. Tracy had eleven points and eight rebounds for the game and Scott Cravens scored ten points. Tracy also guarded Bruce Baker and held him to fifteen points, which was huge for us. I think Benton played all right, but showed some signs that they were going to be a lot better by the time we would see them again in January.

The win over Benton was big for us, but Coach Lee made sure we did not get complacent. We were all happy with the win, but we practiced Monday focused on getting ready for our next opponent and our first home game versus the Norris City Omaha Cardinals.

One funny story after the Benton win happened at practice on the following Monday. Before practice started, Coach Lee gathered us all together and he had a bouquet of red roses. The roses had a card that read:

*Congratulations to Coach Lee and the team for a superb victory over Benton.*

*Some West Frankfort Redbird fans.*

This shows the kind of rivalry that Frankfort and Benton had back at that time.

I was definitely fouled by either Randy House or Bruce Baker in our game at SIU Arena against the Benton Rangers. Daren Carlisle (31) and Kai Nurnberger (20) look on.

Brian Sloan and Benton's Bruce Baker on the cover of the
Southern Illinois Tip Off Classic Program.

30

Coach Lee shows us the bouquet of flowers sent to us by some West Frankfort Redbird fans after we beat the Benton Rangers at the SIU Tip Off Classic.

# 7

# Game 3: Foxes 73 Norris City-Omaha
# Cardinals 48 Foxes 3-0

Our third game of the season was against Norris City-Omaha and would be our first home game. It was no surprise that the gym was packed. The old MHS gym was a pit. It was very old and small. It was not a great place for visiting teams to play when I was at MHS. Fans sitting in the first row could literally put their feet in bounds when the ball was in play. We could squeeze about 2200 people in the gym when the stage was open for seating and all eight of our home games that year were sold out.

Playing NCO was bittersweet for me because I knew some of the players like Carl Peas and Glenn Hall pretty well. My stepmom, Ann Morris, was a graduate of Norris City-Omaha High School and her parents lived next to the NCO head coach, Dave Gray. When I was a kid, I spent a lot of time shooting baskets in Coach Gray's backyard with his son, Clay.

I was a huge fan of Coach Gray's teams in the late 70s, and they had some great ones. I still remember the starters for the 78-79 team that consisted of Cal Johnson, Jeff McKenzie, Mark Wheeler, Mike Minor, and Pat Bain. My dad had officiated several games for Coach Gray and even called the two Eldorado Tournament Title games in 1977 and 1978 when the Cardinals lost to Cairo both years.

I used to joke with Dave that I was sure he was mad that the guy who officiated those games was sleeping in the house next to him after they lost. Dave told me once that my dad tried to help his team get into overtime in the 1979 EHT Title game against Cairo. Cairo was up 54-52 on NCO with just a few seconds left and Norris City-Omaha recovered a loose ball. Dad blew the whistle for a timeout before Coach Gray could even signal. Dad knew Dave was calling for the timeout and 'saved' the Cardinals a second on the clock. Unfortunately, Rick Chappelle had to throw the ball the length of the floor, hit the speaker hanging from the ceiling, and the Cairo Pilots were EHT champs again.

The game against NCO was a blowout. We led 38-23 at the half and 55-29 after the third quarter. This game would be like a lot of the games we would play this year. Our starters and Bryan Cross played very little if any of the fourth quarter and Coach Lee was able to let our bench players get some time. The final score was 73-48. Tracy Sturm led us with twenty points, Scott Cravens had fourteen, Brian scored eleven, Stacy had nine, Bryan Cross had six and I chipped in eight points. Ernie Shelton scored three and Tony Rubenacker scored two.

***Glen Hall, Norris City-Omaha, Guard:*** *I remember Brian Sloan had like twenty points and twenty-one rebounds, and at the end of the game you all were trying to get him a dunk by throwing lobs to him. Our center was Mike McCormick....all 5'11 of him. Toward the end of the game Ernie Shelton was guarding me, along with Tim Biggerstaff, and Ernie smacked me in the mouth pretty hard. He came up after the game and said, 'Sorry man.' I knew them from running cross country. They were laughing about it.*

*I remember we lost by like twenty-five points and later in the year you guys got better and beat teams like Evansville Bosse. I was at all your post-season games after the regional and recall getting pretty damned tired of hearing 'Put Another Log on the Fire.' I never was much of a country fan and that just sealed my hatred of it.*

***Erik Griffin, Carrier Mills, forward:*** *UGGGHHH!!! That damn song!*

***Glen Hall, NCO:*** *And someone would walk out in front of you guys when you came on the floor with a large, green log with your record in white numbers with the win total up to that game. I wanted to burn that damn log.*

***Dave Gray, NCO Head Coach:*** *Our center was Mike McCormick, and he was only about 5'11. He was really strong and athletic. He ran track and won the 'Fat Man 100' at the Christopher Relays later that spring. I told him not to worry about getting any rebounds, but to just box out Sloan and let the other guys try to get the ball.*

*In the regional, that year we played West Frankfort at their place in the semifinals and the winner was going to take on your team. Before the game, I saw that Jim Collins and Kenny Hungate were on the game. Before we took the floor to warm up I told our team that I challenged any of them to foul out of this game because I knew that Hungate and Collins would let us play.*

*Our players beat the Redbird's best player, Don Peavey, to death that game. A couple of players even said they could not believe what they were getting away with at halftime. I don't think we had anybody with more than two fouls in the game. Unfortunately, our strategy worked against us because the game was tied and Glenn Hall drove to the basket for the game-winner, got undercut and Hungate called a charge. We lost on a last-second shot by two points and the Redbirds moved on to face you guys in the regional final.*

It was nice to get to see guys like seniors Ernie Shelton, Tony Rubenacker, and Heath Lasswell, get to play in a game. Those guys, along with our junior varsity players, played an important role in our success that season. They came to practice every day and battled us. Ernie and I went at it every day. Ernie was not very big, but he played hard and made me a better player. People don't give them enough credit for how much they meant to our team.

Scott Cravens scores against Norris City-Omaha in our third game of the season.

The program from our game against the NCOE Cardinals.
The graphics were ahead of their time.

# 8

## Game 4: Foxes at Eldorado Eagles Foxes 54 Eldorado Eagles 46 Foxes 4-0

During the time I played at MHS, we had multiple teams that were considered rivals. Benton and the Carmi Bulldogs were two big rivals, but the Eldorado Eagles were our most bitter rival. I knew Randy House at Benton and Ben Winter, Stacy Woolsey, and a few other Carmi guys always came to the Sloan, Lee, Reed summer camps. We competed hard against each other, but we also respected them as players and people. Eldorado was different than those teams. I think the players really disliked each other.

Eldorado and McLeansboro had some really great battles in the 70s and 80s. Eldorado High School was in the midst of three straight trips to the state tourney when Coach Lee took the job at MHS in 1975. David had a losing record in his first year, but by his third year, MHS was beating Eldorado regularly.

My freshman year, Eldorado had a really good team and beat McLeansboro three times before they came to MHS in February and the Foxes won in one of the most intense games of the season. In 82-83, MHS won all three games and ended the Eagles' season in the sectional semifinals at West Frankfort 72-69. Eldorado had several seniors in 82-83 and was led by Mike Watson, Jeff Melton, and Bill Bradley. In the sectional game, Bill Bradley was ejected from the game for trying to take Darin Lee's head off late in the fourth quarter. My dad, Steve Morris, was the official who ejected Bradley from the game (I was a student at Woodlawn, so Dad was put in that sectional.)

In the first game with Eldorado, we were heavily favored. Eldorado only had one player, Greg Goodley, who had played much at all the year before. However, when the Foxes and Eagles play the records and players are not as important as the rivalry. We knew Eldorado would be ready and Coach Hosman would have a game plan to keep them competitive.

Eldorado played us tough during this game. They led 10-8 after a quarter and we led 24-18 at half. The game was close throughout and we ended up winning 54-46. I have to give Coach Hosman and the Eagles credit. They played us as tough as anyone. Tracy led us with nineteen points and Brian chipped in eleven.

Eldorado played a very deliberate style that night and slowed us down. A lot of people think that we played a slowdown game at MHS because after David left MHS in 1985 to take the job at West Frankfort, Curt Reed was named the head coach. The talent level dropped a bit in Curt's first year or so and he used a lot of slower tactics to be competitive. Curt was known for playing 'Voo Doo ball' as the years passed. I have to remind people that when I was playing, we did not hold the ball on teams…they held the ball on us. Or at least they tried.

I played terribly. They did a great job on Brian and made things tough for thirty-two minutes.

Coach Lee was quoted in the *Times-Leader* saying, "I shouldn't say this because Benton was playing their first game when we beat them and they may eat us alive when we play them again, but Eldorado played better half-court defense than Benton. We got the ball to Brian easily against Benton and the kids thought it would be like that all year long. They found out differently tonight."

It was a good learning experience for us, and I think it was one of the few times we might have overlooked or taken a team lightly.

Coach Lee added, "This was a good learning game for us, especially since we won. When you lose kids get down and don't learn as much."

Coach was disappointed in us for not taking it to the Eagles and I knew that the next few practices were not going to be fun.

Another interesting story is that in 1986, Joe Hosman left Eldorado to take the head coaching job at Massac County High School in Metropolis, IL. I was the head coach at Vienna High School from 1991-95 and we played Massac every year. In 1996, I left Vienna to become the assistant principal at Massac County and worked with Joe. We talked a lot about basketball, and I gained a lot of respect for how hard Joe worked as the coach at MCHS.

# 9

## Game 5: Foxes 60 Carmi Bulldogs 44
## Foxes 5-0

Our next game we traveled about twenty miles east to play the Carmi Bulldogs. Carmi had a very good team under coach Randy Goin led by senior Todd Rice and juniors, Kelly Ackerman, Ben Winter, and Stacy Woolsey. Carmi was better than Eldorado and I think we knew we had to play better than we did against the Eagles, or we were going to lose.

This was the first game where we used our 1-2-2 zone press for a majority of the game and it would prove to be a pivotal part of our season. Our ¾ court press was lethal. I played the point, and Scott Cravens and Tracy Sturm were on the wings. Our press was very passive, and we would lull teams into getting trapped right across half-court. We used our press to jump out to an 18-2 lead on Carmi and really never looked back. Brian led us with twenty points, and we were able to sit our starters for most of the fourth quarter. The score of this game was like a lot of scores in that the game was not that close as the final score might have indicated, but Coach Lee was never one to run the score up on anyone.

**Stacy Woolsey, Carmi Bulldog's Guard:** *Our coach, Randy Goin, was teammates with David Lee at SIU-C, so Ben Winter, Kelly Ackerman,* *and I rode from Carmi to McLeansboro for nine straight summers to attend the Sloan, Lee, Reed Camp at MHS gym.*

*Miserable memories from that game. Lol. Coach Goin told me at halftime in front of the whole team if he had anyone that could bring the ball up the floor my ass would be sitting the bench. Thank God we didn't have anybody else to dribble the ball. You and Cravens picked me apart like piranhas on a bluegill. And Ben Winter was no help at all!!*

*I wish they would have had shootouts like they do now. A game in 1983 between Lawrenceville and Marty Simmons at the 'Foxes Den' against McLeansboro would have been fun to watch.*

# 10

## Game 6: Foxes 63 Carrier Mills Wildcats 42
## Foxes 6-0

Carrier Mills came to play at our place for our sixth game and second home game. I believe that this was the point in our season where our team was really starting to gain a lot of chemistry and all of us were starting to understand how good we could be.

Growing up and watching the Carrier Mills Wildcats, then coached by Jeff Richey, was one of my favorite memories of Southern Illinois basketball. Carrier Mills always seemed to get overlooked, but they were usually talented. I also loved their uniforms. They were one of the last schools to wear jerseys that were untucked, like the 1977 Marquette Warriors and 1980 DePaul Blue Demons. Their 1979 Elite Eight team had terrific players like John 'Hootie' Brown, Steve Evans, Ronnie Williams, and David Taborn and I enjoyed watching them play when I had the chance.

Carrier Mills was coached by Bobby Lane and was 4-2. They had a talented, but very young team. Their leading scorer was senior John Dooley, but two of their best players were a 6'5 freshman Erik Griffin and 6'2 freshman Jody Van Meter.

Once again, we used our 1-2-2 press to blitz Carrier Mills. They had no chance to compete with us on this night. We led 23-4 after the first period and 33-14 at the half. We ended up winning by a score of 63-42. Brian led us with seventeen points and Tracy and Scott pitched in sixteen and fifteen each. However, the most important part of this game was our defense and specifically, Scott Cravens.

*Erik Griffin, Carrier Mills Wildcats' Forward: I spent more of the first quarter at halfcourt watching Morris, Cravens, and Sturm shoot layups off the press. One of our starting guards was hurt and could not play. Honestly, I don't know if he was really hurt or did not want any part of those guys. All I know for sure is that it was the wrong night for my first start as a freshman. I think the biggest cheer from the Foxes' fans was when we finally crossed half-court.*

Scott completely shut down John Dooley. Dooley did not score a point until late in the first half when Scott was on the bench. I also recall the Van Meter kid kind of went after Scott on a layup and Scott was not happy. I grabbed Scott and said, "Scott, don't do it. You will kill him." I think I saved that kid's life that night.

*Erik Griffin: I remember Jody kept getting the ball against the press and was frustrated. He went after Cravens pretty hard on a foul and likely just pissed him off. I think that foul just prolonged the ass-whipping we got that night.*

Scott was a tenacious defender. When we played teams with good guards, we knew that Scott would be one guarding their best perimeter players. Scott deserves a lot of credit for being so unselfish. When he played at Dahlgren Grade School, he averaged about 35 ppg in eighth grade. Scott was about the same size in eighth grade as he was as a senior, so he was bigger and stronger than everyone. Even though he did not grow much, he evolved into a great guard and one of the best defensive players I have ever seen.

Stacy Sturm goes up for two against Carrier Mills.

# 11

## Game 7: Foxes 72 Fairfield Mules 60
## Foxes 7-0

This was another game in which the score was not indicative of how well we played. For the third game in a row, we came out in our 1-2-2 press and then back in our suffocating man-to-man, half-court defense. We jumped out on Fairfield early and the score after three quarters was 61-38. Brian scored twenty points in a little over three-quarters of action. Tracy and Scott both scored fourteen points. Coach Lee cleared the bench early in the fourth quarter and allowed Ernie Shelton, Tony Rubenacker, Heath Lasswell, Jim Melton, Tim Biggerstaff, and the rest of the players to get some time on the floor.

I do remember that we were a little ticked off that Fairfield scored sixty points in the game. It would be the only time all year that a team would score sixty points or more against us.

The first part of the season was complete. We were playing pretty well, and we were 7-0 heading into the Eldorado Holiday Tournament as the #1 seed. However, Brian, Tracy, and Scott had carried a majority of the scoring load for us up to this point. It was time for Stacy, Bryan Cross, and me to start to contribute more, especially against good teams.

One thing a lot of people did not realize about Stacy, Cross and I was that we were really young for our grade. All three of us were born in summer 1967. Lots of parents would have held their kids back so that they would have been a year later in school, but our parents did not do that. The three of us could have all been sophomores during the 83-84 season.

*David Lee: I had a key to the local cable TV building that housed the cable equipment for McLeansboro. Each Sunday, my stepson, DL, and I would take the VHS tape of the game(s) to the building and DL would put the tape in the cable system so that anyone that had cable could watch the game(s) again from the previous week. It was amazing how many people said that they watched the game again on Sunday afternoon. The community was totally involved with the team.*

A collage of pics from our game against Fairfield at home.
We would beat the Mules 72-60.

Tracy Sturm with a reverse layup against the Fairfield Mules.

# 12

# *The Eldorado Holiday Tournament*

The Eldorado Holiday Tournament was one of the best holiday tournaments and perhaps the best small school Holiday tournament in Illinois during the 70s, 80s, and early 90s. I had the good fortune of growing up around the EHT when my dad was coaching at Eldorado High School from 1974-77. I attended every EHT game from 1974-1980. That was twenty-three games in three days from 9:00 a.m. until about midnight each day...and I loved every second of it. Dad would get me a scorebook and I would keep score of every game.

I watched great players like Eldorado, Mike Duff, Barry Smith, Eddie Lane, Otha Watkins, and Harvey 'Juice' McNeal from Cairo, all the Taborns from Carrier Mills, Norman and Ronny Goodman from Metropolis, Keil Peebles from Johnston City, and many others. One of my greatest memories is the first EHT I ever attended. Metropolis was the #1 seed and played Johnston City in the first semifinal. Harrisburg had a really good team with their best player, Joe Culbreth, and played Eldorado in the second semifinal.

Metropolis beat Johnston City in double overtime. Keil Peebles was incredible in that game. He hit a jumper from about forty feet to send the game to the second overtime, but the Trojans held on. Eldorado beat Harrisburg, their Saline County rival, in the second game by one point.

This meant that Metropolis and Eldorado would play in the championship that night.

I had never seen so many people at a game. It was impossible to walk through the upper concourse of Duff-Kingston that night because it was a standing-room-only crowd. People smoked in the gym in those days and a cloud formed above the court from all the people lighting up at the game. I remember sitting under the scorer's table during the game. Metropolis won 55-52 in a great championship and, even though I was crushed that the Eagles lost, I was hooked. I wanted to play in the EHT someday.

Leading up to the tournament we were seeded #1 and heavily favored. I don't think there was a clear #2 team, but the other top four seeds were Massac County, DuQuoin, and Carmi. The tournament was not quite as strong as previous years because Meridian and Cairo both left to go to the Carbondale Holiday Tournament at SIU Arena. In any case, we knew we would still be challenged.

Our first opponent would be the Anna-Jonesboro Wildcats. AJ was known more as a football school but still had some talent. We prepared for them before Christmas break and then took off for Christmas Day. Around Christmas Day the Midwest got hit by a record snowstorm. The EHT got pushed back a day. We had a rule that if we ever had a snow day, practice was at 1 p.m. and just get there as soon as possible. A lot of our players lived in rural Hamilton County. Stacy and Tracy lived near Macedonia. Cravens and Cross lived around Dahlgren, and I lived south of McLeansboro about a mile off the highway. The road to my house was impassable. I ended up riding to practice on a snowmobile. Somehow, we all got to the gym.

The worst part of the storm was a pipe had burst in our locker room and was flooded. A number of us had our game shoes ruined. Tracy and Stacy Sturm brought in a bunch of old basketball shoes that they had at their house and some of us used their shoes for practice. After practice, my stepdad and I drove to Mt Vernon and bought me a new pair of Nike basketball shoes. My family did not have a lot of money, so getting a new pair of basketball shoes was a big deal. My shoes that were in the flooding actually ended up being fine, but I started playing well in my new ones, so I never changed the rest of the season.

*Stacy Sturm: I remember before the EHT, we had to practice in a cold gym with no heat because of the snowstorm that hit the Midwest that winter. But the coaches brought us donuts to eat after practice.*

# 13

# Game 8: Foxes 85 Anna-Jonesboro 45
# Foxes 8-0

Walking into the back entrance of Duff-Kingston for our first game of the EHT brought back so many great memories for me. The smell of the gym and the locker rooms reminds me of when my kid's mom and I would drop our daughter off to ride her horse, Polly. Chloe would get out of the car and pause for a moment, then take a deep breath and say, "God, I love that smell." Duff-Kingston did the same thing for me with the smell of musty locker rooms, new basketballs, and the coffee, donuts, and cold-cut sandwiches in the hospitality room.

Generally, the #1 team in a tournament plays the worst team. I was surprised A-J was our opening opponent. They had some good athletes and a great coach in Mike Crews. Mike was still the coach at A-J when I coached at Vienna High School from 1991-95 and we became good friends. He was a great coach, but also one of the funniest human beings I have known. Mike was asked before the 1991-92 season what was the key for his team's upcoming season and he responded with, "Graduation!"

A-J also had a former Fox playing for them in junior Joel Reed. Joel had attended McLeansboro from about third-seventh grade while his dad, Lew Reed, was coaching football at MHS. Joel was a really good athlete and we had been friends growing up. He moved to Flora in eighth grade and then came back for his freshman and sophomore years. He moved to A-J for his junior year, and I remember thinking he could have helped us during the season and for sure when we would be seniors.

We played well against A-J. The score at the end of the first quarter was 25-13. The second quarter A-J played well and outscored us 18-17. We led 41-30 at the half and I recall that Coach Lee was not happy and lit into us at the half. We came out in the third quarter and went after the Wildcats with our 1-2-2 press and man-to-man pressure in half-court. We outscored A-J 26-6 in the third and led 67-36 after three quarters. We also ran K-State for Brian, and he hammered a monster dunk before the end of the quarter. Coach Lee cleared the bench and we won 85-45.

Brian Sloan hammering home a dunk against the A-J Wildcats in the EHT.

Scott Cravens takes a shot against the A-J Wildcats in
our opening game of the 1983 EHT.

# 14

## Game 9: Foxes 58 Trico Pioneers 33
## Foxes 9-0

In the second game of the tournament, we faced the Trico Pioneers. This was the first year Trico had been in the tourney, and we did not know much about them other than they had some size. Trico's best player was 6'7 Bruce Prange and Coach Lee made sure we knew he was really good. It was a fairly methodical game for us as Trico hung around for a bit. The score was 13-8 at the end of the first quarter. Prange picked up his third foul in the second quarter and we slowly pulled away. The score at the half was 31-20. We led 43-28 after three quarters and ended up winning 58-33. Tracy led us with twenty points, Brian had sixteen points and eleven boards, and Cravens pitched in ten. Once again, Coach Lee was able to clear the bench and get everyone in the game before it was over.

Scott Cravens gets challenged by multiple Trico defenders as
he goes up for a layup in the EHT.

Stacy Sturm loses the ball against Trico in the second round of the EHT. We did not make many mistakes in the tourney as we rolled to the title in dominating fashion.

# 15

## Game 10: Foxes 59 Eldorado Eagles 37
## Foxes 10-0

The four teams in the semifinals were McLeansboro, Harrisburg, Christopher, and Eldorado. All three of the other teams that made it to the semifinals were unseeded heading into the tournament. The first semifinal game was the Harrisburg Bulldogs vs the Christopher Bearcats. Harrisburg upset DuQuoin and Christopher upset Massac County in the quarterfinals. A lot of teams might have had a letdown knowing that the other top seeds were out, but we were a pretty mature group and our coaches made sure we were focused. The game against Eldorado earlier in the season had taught us that we were a beatable team if we did not play hard all the time.

Personally, I was happy that Christopher had made it to the semifinals because I knew their head coach, Tom Wheeler, his wife, Lynda, and his family very well. Coach Wheeler was a former Fox, and I was also dating Coach Wheeler's daughter, Dhana, during the season. I also knew his son TJ, who would go on to set the scoring record at the EHT in 1990 and play at Illinois. I actually spent a lot of time around Coach Wheeler when he was playing softball in the summers with my dad.

Coach Lee did not get us to the game very early. When we played in tournaments, we generally arrived in time to go straight to the locker room and get ready for the game. We did not see any of the first semifinals, but Harrisburg won a close game over the Bearcats. Now we were ready for the rematch with Eldorado.

I remember sitting in the Duff-Kingston Gymnasium locker room and thinking about winning this game. I was not going to play like I did in the first game, which was very passive. Eldorado had a reputation for being very aggressive and, sometimes, even dirty. They also talked a lot of trash. Shawn Pilkington had said a bunch of stuff about my dad during the first game and I let it bother me. This game was going to be different.

In the first game, Pilkington and Greg Goodley hurt us from the outside. In this game, we held them to a combined seven points. The game was really never in doubt, and we ended up winning 59-37. Tracy led us with twenty-three points and Brian chipped in nineteen.

Once again, Coach Lee cleared the bench early in the fourth quarter and everyone got some time. One of the most memorable things that happened was with Mark Snyder. Mark was a great teammate and helped keep things light with our team. He always led our team in the most times grabbing the rim during practice. Mark got in with about a minute to go and as the clock was running down, he hit a twenty-five-foot jumper at the buzzer. It was one of the few times that we got excited at the end of a blowout. All of us on the bench jumped up and went out to 'the Snyde.' It was a great moment for Mark and all of us.

Scott Cravens goes up for a basket against the Eldorado Eagles in the semifinals of the EHS. Scott could have averaged 18-20 points a game, but he was so unselfish and willing to sacrifice his offense for the team. However, he never sacrificed his defense. Scott was tenacious guarding opposing players.

# 16

## Game 11: Foxes 58 Harrisburg Bulldogs 51
## Foxes 11-0

Since we were playing two games in one day, we went to a local motel in Eldorado to rest before the championship game. We had about four hours or so to relax and get ready for Harrisburg. I was in a room with Tracy Sturm. We did not say much about the game. We watched some college basketball and rested. I spent my time thinking about how much I wanted to win this game. I had grown up around the EHT and dreamed of 'cutting down the nets' after winning the title. I usually thought about scoring thirty points and hitting the game-winner at the buzzer, but I was pretty sure that neither of those things were going to happen.

We left the hotel about 5:00 p.m. to go eat dinner and then returned for our pregame talk about Harrisburg. We always knew that Coach Lee would have us ready with a scouting report. Coach Reed usually went over the other team, and this was also one of the few times during the season that our freshman coach, Randy Smithpeters, was on the bench.

Randy was usually scouting during the season when he was not coaching the freshman. People don't have a real understanding of the sacrifices Randy made for us by spending two or three nights a week on the road scouting our next opponent. Coaches today have access to video of teams via the internet, but we did not have that luxury. Randy spent a lot of nights away from his wife and his sons, Kolby and Kyle, so that we could be prepared for each game. Randy would eventually become the head coach at Harrisburg in the early 90s and his 2013 team won the Illinois Class 2A State Title.

About an hour before the championship game, the team met in the coach's room. They had taken all the pictures off the walls. This was a pretty cheap hotel and had old, brown paneling on the walls. Coach Reed had written the scouting report for each player and what their team did on the wall in chalk. It was pretty funny to see.

We were not going to overlook Harrisburg. They did not have a great record, but they had some really good athletes and played in the South Seven conference against a lot of really good AA schools like Carbondale, Centralia, Marion as well as the Benton Rangers. Harrisburg had one of the top football programs in the state. My dad and I used to go to their playoff games, and I knew their previous football coach, Ken Joggerst, and their head coach at that time, Al Way, pretty well. Dad played a lot of softball with Coach Joggerst and Al Way was the head football coach at Eldorado for the last two years Dad was at EHS.

Harrisburg was coached by Tony Holler. I did not know Coach Holler very well, but when I went on to play ball at the University of Wisconsin-Superior I played for Glenn Carlson, who was a good friend of Coach Holler's. Harrisburg had some size and athleticism. Adrian Lanton and Scott Boyd were both about 6'4 and I had played against them as a freshman on the junior varsity team. Scott Williams was a solid guard and Phil Shelton was a sophomore who would go on to become an outstanding player by the end of his career.

I don't think any of the players knew, but this would be the first time since 1968 that the Foxes would play in the championship game. McLeansboro won the tournament in 1968 and had not made it to the finals since. In fact, the Foxes did not make it to the semifinals again until 1980. In 1980, the Foxes lost a close game to Cairo in the semifinals and finished third. In 1981, McLeansboro entered the tourney unseeded but beat top-rated Cairo in the quarterfinals. They lost to a really talented DuQuoin Indians' team led by the late Darrel Anders and finished third again.

In 1982, the Foxes were seeded fourth and lost a heartbreaking game to Cairo 64-62 in a very controversial ending. MHS was down two with one second left and the ball under their own basket. They had to go the full length of the court to get a tying basket. Coach Lee drew up the last play and Tracy Sturm caught the ball at half-court. Tracy turned and took a shot from about forty-five feet as the buzzer sounded. The ball went in, and it was bedlam. McLeansboro's fans went crazy thinking the game was going to overtime. Cairo and their coach, Bill Chumbler, went crazy thinking the buzzer went off before Tracy released the ball. I watched the tape and could not hear the horn. One of the guys on the score bench fired a starter pistol. Coach Lee and Coach Chumbler were both at center court pleading their case to the officials. After a few minutes, the officials waved off the basket. Coach Lee was livid. In the end, after watching the tape over and over, I think they got the call correct.

Back at the hotel, we boarded the bus and headed to the gym thinking the third-place game between Christopher and Eldorado would almost be over. When we got to the gym, the crowd was going crazy. The third-place game was a real battle and ended up going to three overtimes. I was rooting for Coach Wheeler and the Bearcats because he was a great guy (and he let me date his daughter) and because they were playing Eldorado. Sadly, the Bearcats lost to Eldorado in triple overtime.

We finally took the floor for the title game and the gym was packed. In the mid-70s and early 80s, one thing you could guarantee was the EHT championship game would be sold out. This night was no different and we saw for the first time the 'Green Wave' of fans from Hamilton County coming out in droves. I think people began to sense something special was building.

The title game was really anticlimactic. The quote in the *Times-Leader* was we won despite an 'uninspired effort.' We jumped out to an early lead and led by double figures at half. In the third quarter, we built up close to a twenty-point lead. In the huddle, before the fourth quarter started, Coach Lee set up a play against Harrisburg's 1-3-1 defense to get Brian a dunk off a lob. We ran the play, and I threw a lob to Brian. Brian jumped and just hammered a dunk attempt, but the ball rattled out.

We were up fifteen in the fourth and Coach Lee emptied the bench. Everyone got in and we ended up winning 58-51. Brian led us with twenty points and six boards, Scott had a great game with eighteen points, and Tracy finished with sixteen. The score was not indicative of how well we played. All four of our wins in the EHT were blowouts and likely the most dominant run since Eldorado in the 1975 tournament. Brian was named MVP and Tracy was named First Team All-Tournament. I was disappointed Scott Cravens did not make the second Team, but he did not care. Scott was like all of us in that he just wanted to win and did not care about individual awards.

After we won there was not a lot of celebration. We were happy to win the tournament, but we also knew we were going to have a target on our back the rest of the season. We were 11-0 and had a few days off before the first of the year. Once 1984 started, we would have four games and then head to the Benton Invitational Tournament. I know I was happy with how we were playing, but I was far from satisfied. I also knew that there were going to be times in the future where Bryan Cross, Stacy Sturm and I were going to have to step up because Sloan, Cravens, and Tracy Sturm were going to get a lot of attention from teams.

The 1983 EHT All-Tourney team. Tracy Sturm was named 1st team and Brian Sloan was the MVP. Scott Cravens should have been named all-tourney as well, but he never said a word. We did not care about individual awards and honors. All we wanted to do was win.

The 1983 Eldorado Holiday Tournament Champs!!! McLeansboro's first EHT in fifteen years. Our average margin of victory in the four games was almost 25ppg.

Tracy Sturm goes up for two points against the Harrisburg Bulldogs in the title game of the EHT.

# 17

## Game 12: Foxes 68 Christopher Bearcats 40
## Foxes 12-0

After a few days off, we returned to practice to get ready for the Christopher Bearcats. Christopher was playing very well coming off their surprising run in the EHT. They had some very good athletes who were probably better football players and track athletes than basketball players, but they had some size and competed hard. Their best players were leading scorer Doug Beleos, Phil Steinmetz, Joe Bullock, and Brent Gossett. They also had the Koropchak twins who were both very physical, 6'3 post players.

It was bittersweet playing against Coach Wheeler. 'Wheels', as he is better known, is one of the best people I know and also a huge fan of Southern Illinois sports. Tom and his wife, Lynda, have lived in Buckner, a very small town between Christopher and Benton, in the same house for over forty years. Tom has a building, called Tom's Garage, next to his house that is filled with press clippings, photos, and other memorabilia from Southern Illinois sports over the last fifty years or so. Coach Wheeler was one of the first people I contacted when I thought about writing this book because I knew he had lots of memorabilia from the 83-84 season. Tom is one of the most well-known and respected coaches in the history of Southern Illinois sports.

Tom was a very unique coach in that he never cut anyone from his teams. Tom told me once he did not believe in cutting kids and would keep any kid who came out. I always thought that was pretty cool. I also remember his junior varsity teams having like twenty-five kids sitting on the bench during their games. I was lucky to get to know the Wheelers and also to play for Tom for two years at RLC and then coach with him at RLC as well.

> **Tom Wheeler:** *I actually did have one rule for cutting kids and that was 'cuts based on haircuts.' Kids had to get a nice, flattop haircut to get a uniform.*
>
> *We eventually had so many kids on our freshman team, that we had to add a game to let everyone play. We had an 'A game' for the best freshmen players, then a 'B game' for the next group. I started a 'Splinter Game' for the rest of the kids to play. The kids in the Splinter game brought both uniforms to every game and we would have an intrasquad game between the last twelve to fifteen players on the bench. The fans and players loved the Splinter game because those kids were not very skilled, but they played their hearts out.*

All of our players knew Wheels and his son, TJ, very well. Tom had a youth program at CHS called 'Little Wheels' that he had developed over the years as the coach at CHS. Wheels had over 500 kids from all over Southern Illinois take part in his Little Wheels program. Tom started the program too late for me to take part in it, but one of my younger brothers, Matt Morris, took part in Little Wheels when he was a kid. That is likely why Matt was a better player than me.

Wheels and TJ also traveled around Southern Illinois speaking at camps in the summer. We all thought TJ was going to be a good player, but we had no idea he would grow to be 6'5 and be one of the all-time leading scorers in the history of Southern Illinois. Then, TJ went on to have a solid career playing at the University of Illinois for Lou Henson. He played with great players like Deon Thomas and against teams like Michigan and the 'Fab Five.' TJ even spent a summer playing for the Chicago Bulls summer league team after he finished playing with the

Illini and was told he would be invited to camp the following fall, but he was not invited and decided it was time to hang up his 'Jordans' rather than go to the CBA and try to hook up with another NBA team.

I also recall going to the Wheeler's later in the year to take Dhana Wheeler to a movie or hang out with their family on the weekends. TJ had made a VCR tape of all the best dunks he could record from TV. We must have watched that tape about 100 times. Wheels quit coaching basketball at Christopher before TJ entered High School but continued to teach at CHS. Wheels ended up taking a job as an assistant coach at Rend Lake College and in the 1985-86 season there were five former Foxes playing for him and Coach Mitch Haskins at RLC.

*Tom Wheeler, Christopher Head Coach: The thing I remember about that game was Brian carrying the EHT Holiday Tournament Trophy out when you guys came out to warm up before the game for all of the fans to see.*

This was another game that was really never in doubt for us. Doug Beleos, the Bearcat's leading scorer and second-team all-tourney at the EHT, did not play. We used our pressure to jump out to an early lead of 21-8 after the first period. The score at the half was 39-18 and Coach Lee cleared the bench early in the fourth period when we were up 61-32. We ended up winning 68-40. Brian led us with twenty-two points and thirteen rebounds, while Stacy and Scott chipped in thirteen each and I scored eight.

*Brad Reynolds, MHS Class of 85: Our fans came out like crazy that year and I did not miss a game. I was with some buddies before the Christopher game, and we knew we had to get to the games early to get a seat in the student section. Well, we got to the gym too late and had to sit on the visitor's side.*

*I started talking trash to the Bearcat fans and said something like, "Tell Rich Herrin on your way home that we are going to kill them next week!!"*

*Some fan said, "If you turn around you can tell Coach Herrin yourself."*

*Little did I know that Coach Herrin was sitting behind me. I turned around and he just smiled at me. It was pretty funny.*

# 18

# Game 13: Foxes 90 Zeigler-Royalton 36 Foxes 13-0

Our next opponent was the Zeigler-Royalton Tornadoes. Even though Z-R did not have a great record, they had one of the top players in the state and nation in Sean Connor. Sean was averaging about 33 ppg at that time of the year. Even though we were expected to win easily, there was a lot of hype with the matchup between future IU Hoosier, Brian Sloan, and Sean. In fact, that night the University of Illinois' top assistant, Dick Nagy, was sitting on the front row with former Illini great and also former Eldorado Eagles' coach, Bob Brown.

There were very few games where Brian said much about our opponent, but Brian was fired up for this game. He was going to guard Sean Connor, and he told me he was going to shut him down. I have never seen someone so pumped about playing defense, but that was Brian.

This game was a total demolition from the start. During the season, there were three games where I believe we played as close to perfect as possible. This was the first of the three. We came out, put our 1-2-2 press on Z-R, and suffocated them. My dad said there was about a two-minute period where the Tornadoes did not cross center court. The score was 24-0 before Z-R finally scored. We were up 31-6 after the first quarter and 56-16 at the half.

Coach Lee said, "It was an unbelievable display by our kids. It wasn't that Z-R was missing shots, they could not get any shots."

*Scott Cravens: I remember Coach Lee challenging us during the Ziegler game to see how long we would shut them out and how many points we could score before they could score. He wanted us to completely shut them down. If I remember correctly, we scored 19 points before they could even start their offense. It was 31-6 at the end of the first quarter.*

I also remember that there were very few times during a timeout that Coach Lee did not have something to tell us that would help us play better. Z-R's coach, Jerry DeNosky, called their last timeout in the second quarter. We were in the huddle and Coach Lee kneeled down in front of us. Brian, Stacy, Tracy, Scott, and I sat on the bench while the other players leaned in to listen to what Coach had to say. David had a habit of taking his partial out and messing with it when he was thinking and that is what he was doing during the timeout.

After about forty-five seconds, David put his partial in his mouth, stuck his hand out, and said, "All right, let's go." It was the only time Coach Lee was ever speechless in my time playing for him.

In the locker room at halftime, Coach Lee could not come up with anything critical to say to us. He went around and told each of us something that we did well in the first half of the game. I had made a nice pass to Scott on the break for a layup and coach said something like, "Jeff, I don't know how you made that pass to Scott on the break." It was a great feeling for us to play so well that David was almost speechless. It wasn't that David did not see how good we were, but he had to make sure we did not get complacent and continued to push us to get better. There were times we made it hard for him to find things to criticize.

I don't want to sound like Coach Lee never said anything positive to us, because he did. But that was the way David coached and he was not unique. A few years after I finished playing at McLeansboro, I ran into a kid who played for Coach Lee at West Frankfort in the late 1980s. We were talking and he told me that he got so tired of hearing about how great of a point guard Jeff Morris was for Coach Lee at MHS. I laughed and asked what David had said about me. He told me that all he heard was, 'If Jeff Morris was in practice, he would kick your ass all over this gym!' or 'You could not come close to being as tough as Jeff was when he played for me!" I got a chuckle out of that and assured him that when I played, I was one of the worst players on two of the worst teams David ever had and we were 59-6 my two years with a state title.

Coach Lee ended up clearing the bench in the third quarter and the rest of the players got some well-deserved floor time. Brian dropped in thirty points and twelve rebounds, Tracy had twenty-four and nine, Cravens chipped in thirteen, and I finished with eight and five. We also out-rebounded Z-R 52-18 for the game. Brian played great, but his proudest part of the game was holding Sean Connor to eight points through three quarters. Sean ended up scoring ten points in the fourth quarter to finish with eighteen for the game. I remember feeling a bit sorry for what Sean had to go through that night, but he ended up having a great career and played basketball for Digger Phelps at Notre Dame.

This would be our last home game for a month. We had a really tough road trip the following weekend to Massac County on Friday night and DuQuoin on Saturday. Even though they had both been upset at the EHT, we knew traveling over an hour on consecutive nights and playing two good teams was going to be tough. After we shook hands with the players from Z-R, we were walking off the floor and Coach Lee did something that I will always remember because it showed how far he was thinking ahead.

Coach Lee got on the microphone and asked the fans to stay for a few minutes. David thanked them for supporting us, filling our gym every night, and taking the 'Green Wave' on the road with us. Then, Coach Lee told them that we would have a really tough road trip this weekend and then go on to the Benton Invitational Tournament the following week. David asked them to come out for the games because we needed them for the next few weeks more than ever. It was a genius move on Coach Lee's part.

Brian goes up for a dunk off of a lob against the Z-R Tornadoes.

Scott Cravens scores at the Ziegler-Royalton Tornadoes.

# 19

## Game 14: Foxes 66 Massac County Patriots 53 Foxes 14-0

The first game of our weekend road trip was to Metropolis, IL to face the Massac County Patriots. Massac County was in its third year of existence after Brookport high school and Metropolis High School consolidated in 1981. Massac had a very talented and young team with good size and athleticism. Their best players were 6'3 senior center, Chris Sutton, 6'4 junior guard, Kemble Smith, and 6'3 junior forward, Bruce Wilcox. We were prepared for a very difficult game against the Patriots.

The Patriots were coached by Steve Woodward. 'Woody', as he was called, had been the coach at Metropolis/MCHS for about a decade and had some very talented teams during his time as head coach. In 1995, I left Vienna high school to take a job as assistant principal at MCHS, and Woody and I had offices next to each other. At that time, he was serving only as the athletic director. Steve was very innovative and was one of the first athletic directors to start hosting 'shootouts' at a High School.

In the mid-90s, Woody started the Superman Shootout hosted by MCHS. He brought in the best teams from Illinois, Kentucky, and Missouri along with nationally ranked schools like Oak Hill Academy to play all day at the MCHS gym. Steve eventually would retire and move on to Marshall County high school in Kentucky and move the shootout to their gym. The shootouts Steve created were really the first of their kind in the tri-state area and maybe even the nation.

Our game with the Patriots was close throughout. The gym was packed and, even though we had a great following, the folks from Massac were very loud and trying to help their team upset us. The first quarter ended with us ahead 17-16 and we led at the half 32-27. Brian was in foul trouble most of the game and had to sit out much of the second quarter. However, this allowed Stacy Sturm to show what he could do, and he was terrific. Stacy carried us on the inside and finished the game with thirteen points and six boards. We slowly pulled away in the third quarter and led by ten going into the fourth period. Brian managed to stay on the floor until fouling out late in the game.

We ended up winning a very tough game 66-53. There were two reasons we won that game. First, Stacy played great while Brian was on the bench in the second quarter. The second reason was we outrebounded the Patriots 34-13 and shot almost 68% from the floor for the game. Brian led us with twenty-four points and eleven rebounds, Cravens had fourteen and Tracy finished with eleven. It was the first time all year we had four players in double figures in the same game. It was a tough game, and we were lucky to get out of Massac with a win.

***David Lee:*** *After the Massac County game at their place, I started to believe that we might win every game on the rest of the schedule. I never went into a game thinking we would lose. Practices were very hard for a purpose. I knew hard practices would ready us for every team. As the undefeated season progressed, people would ask me if I thought we needed a loss. I never thought we needed a loss because our players were not overconfident and "big-headed". They were just prepared and confident.*

Coach Lee gets an explanation from the officials during the game against Massac County. This was the first game of a tough week on the road. We beat a good Patriot team 66-53 and would then travel to DuQuoin for another tough opponent the following night.

I attempted a pass against the Massac County Patriots. This play was broken up,
but we ended up winning a tough road game 66-53.

# 20

# Game 15: Foxes 73 DuQuoin Indians 59
# Foxes 15-0

We traveled to face the DuQuoin Indians on Saturday night. This was the first time we had played back-to-back games other than in a tournament. We got home on Friday night at about midnight, so we were going to be a little tired. DuQuoin had a very young team led by one of the top sophomores in the state in 6'4 Monte Kuhnert. Monte had started as a freshman and would end up being one of the leading scorers in the history of Southern Illinois basketball.

Once again, the game was very tight and also called very tight by the officials. Our team was in foul trouble all night long. The teams combined for forty-six fouls and sixty-five free throw attempts. Brian had what was probably his worst game of the year because of foul trouble.

We led at the end of the first quarter 13-12. DuQuoin decided not to guard me during the game and, to be honest, it made sense. I had not scored in double figures in a game all year. Coach Lee told me to step up and shoot the ball if they left me open and that was what I did. In the second quarter, I made a few open jumpers and free throws to get into double figures and that helped us build a 31-20 lead at the half.

***Monte Kuhnert, DuQuoin, All-State Forward:*** *I was a sophomore that year and went against Brian. Had to shoot a lot of rainbows over him. We hung in pretty well, but you guys were so good. I was at the state tourney in 83 and 84 after you all won. We were at the hotel after you guys won the title and Coach Lee got everyone singing* Put Another Log on the Fire. *I became good friends with Brian Sloan and his dad, Jerry. I would see Jerry at the DuQuoin State Fair. I also was good friends with Tracy Sturm. I remember him being interviewed by Coach Bob Dallas after you beat Mt. Pulaski and he said "Thanks, Bob." I was like, man, that is Coach Dallas! Not Bob!*

The second half of the game was crazy. In the third quarter, we continued to build our lead and led 47-30 going in to the fourth quarter. However, we were in serious foul trouble. Brian, Stacy, Tracy, and Scott all had at least three fouls. Brian fouled out with about six minutes left in the game. DuQuion was pressuring us and trying to make the game more up-tempo. In the last half of the fourth quarter, Stacy, Tracy, and Scott all fouled out. With about two minutes left in the game, I was the only starter left in the game. We finished the game with Ernie Shelton, Brian Ingram, Tim Biggerstaff, Crossy and me on the floor.

I remember Coach Lee called me over to the bench while we were shooting free throws and he said, "Jeff, get the ball across half court and you and Crossy play catch till they foul one of you."

It is funny to think about now, but at the time it was our best strategy. DuQuoin outscored us 29-26 in the fourth quarter, but we held on to win 73-59. I led us in scoring with twenty-three points, Scott pitched in nineteen, Tracy had twelve, and Ernie Shelton made a big basket for us and hit two big free throws to finish with four points. Brian had by far his worst game with nine points and five rebounds.

Brian was really down after the game for the way he had played. I felt bad for him, but I also knew that this was a good test for us. We beat a good team with Brian not playing well and four starters fouling out. It was a huge weekend for us to win both games. It was now on to the Benton Invitational Tournament.

Me handling the ball against the DuQuoin Indian's pressure late in the game. At this point, I was the only starter left on the floor due to other starters fouling out. We finished the game with Cross, Ernie Shelton, Tim Biggerstaff, Brian Ingram and me on the floor. We escaped DuQuoin with a 73-59 win to stay unbeaten and finish a tough weekend.

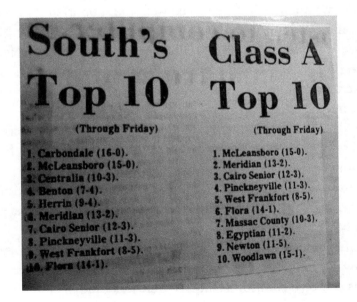

# South's Top 10
### (Through Friday)

1. Carbondale (16-0).
2. McLeansboro (15-0).
3. Centralia (10-3).
4. Benton (7-4).
5. Herrin (9-4).
6. Meridian (13-2).
7. Cairo Senior (12-3).
8. Pinckneyville (11-3).
9. West Frankfort (8-5).
10. Flora (14-1).

# Class A Top 10
### (Through Friday)

1. McLeansboro (15-0).
2. Meridian (13-2).
3. Cairo Senior (12-3).
4. Pinckneyville (11-3).
5. West Frankfort (8-5).
6. Flora (14-1).
7. Massac County (10-3).
8. Egyptian (11-2).
9. Newton (11-5).
10. Woodlawn (15-1).

One of the weekly rankings from the Southern Illinoisan newspaper during the season. We were #1 in class A all year and ended up #1 among all schools by the end of the season.

# 21

# The Fans Become the 'Green Wave'

Our following during the season was amazing. McLeansboro and all of Hamilton County had become renowned in Southern Illinois for people coming out to watch the Foxes play. During the 1982-83 season the fans supported the team all the way through to the third-place finish. So, we knew that if we played well, the support and the expectations would continue.

Once we made it to the BIT undefeated, the number of fans who were wearing green and white at games became overwhelming. Our students were great. Our school only had an enrollment of about 450 kids, but it seemed like 1000 of them were at each game.

We also had fans like Charlie 'Super Fox' Pendell at every game. 'Super Fox' was famous, or maybe infamous to opposing fans, for being loud at our games. He could always be counted on to get the 'F-O-X-E-S' chant started at just the right time. I don't think Charlie missed a game from the time he was in High School in the early seventies until he passed away on December 17, 2017.

I can't name all the fans who supported us because there were just too many. But whether it was people like Dick and Lucille Auten feeding us pizzas or Edgar Johnson giving us Werther's candy before the games, we knew we had a lot of people behind us. MHS and Hamilton County

High School athletes have been lucky to have people like them to help support the programs.

> **Don Lewis:** *My dad was manager at the shirt factory, he cut up a whole bunch of green fabric. He handed them out to the cheerleaders to pass out to the fans. He helped start the green wave!*

# 22

# #1 in the State in Class A

When the first few Associated Press polls came out for Class A basketball, Providence St. Mel was #1 and we were ranked #2. I don't really think any of us thought much about it, but I think there was a bit of a feeling like it was a slap in our face. The week after we beat Massac and DuQuoin the AP poll came out and for the first time in school history, we were #1 in Class A. The rankings for that week were:

| | | |
|---|---|---|
| 1. | McLeansboro | 15-0 (10 first-place votes) |
| 2. | Providence St. Mell | 14-2 (8) |
| 3. | Madison | 10-2 (2) |
| 4. | Toluca | 13-0 |
| 5. | Hamilton | 13-0 |
| 6. | Breese Mater Dei | 13-0 |
| 7. | Beardstown | 13-0 |
| 8. | Mt. Pulaski | 13-1 |
| 9. | Mounds Meridian | 13-1 |
| 10. | Havana | 11-2 |
| 11. | Quincy Notre Dame | 13-2 |
| 12. | Elmhurst IC | 14-2 |
| 13. | Chrisman | 14-0 |

| 14. Ridgewood | 13-0 |
| 15. Flora | 13-1 |
| 16. Ottawa Marquette | 12-3 |

I don't recall the players talking much about being rated #1. We had too much work to do and knew that the rankings had no bearing on what we were trying to accomplish. Coach Lee did not talk to us as a team about being #1, but he did not back down from the ranking when talking to the press. Coach Lee was quoted in the *Times-Leader* saying, "I thought we should have been number 1 right off the bat because of St. Mel's two losses. If you are a competitor, you look for challenges and competition. We'd rather have it that way than the other."

# 23

# The Benton Invitational Tournament (The BIT)

The BIT was not one of the oldest tournaments in Southern Illinois, but it was still very prestigious and had many great teams and players play in it over the years. The first time I attended a game at the BIT was in 1975 when Eldorado played Benton in the semifinals. Benton was loaded that year. They had Bill Smith (Georgia Tech) and Robbie Dunbar (Western Kentucky). The Rangers were undefeated and ranked #1 in Illinois in Class AA. Benton would beat the Eagles and win the BIT over the Olney Tigers in a blowout. Ironically, Rich Herrin, the coach at Benton, went against his brother, Ron, who was the head coach at Olney.

The one thing I remember vividly was seeing Coach Herrin on the sideline. Even then he was a legend and year after year he turned out great teams. I also remember that Coach Herrin and his players had shaved heads. I thought that was pretty cool and kind of intimidating.

I had the good fortune of getting to know both of the Herrin brothers over the years. I had talked to Coach Herrin several times when dad officiated games at Benton. After my playing days were over in college, I came back and served as an assistant coach at Rend Lake College with Ron Herrin. I was lucky to work with Ron for two years before he died in 1997. Rich continued coaching well into his eighties before he passed away in 2020. I can say without reservation that as good as Rich and Ron were as coaches, they were better human beings.

The BIT started as an eight-team, double elimination tournament where the teams were going to play three games in the week of the tourney. In the late 1970s, Coach Herrin decided to change the format of the tournament to a six-team, round-robin format. At that time, there were not any tournaments like that anywhere in the area. It was a genius move on Coach Herrin's part. This meant that six of the top teams in Southern Illinois were going to play five games during the week with a game on Monday, Wednesday, Friday, and two games on Saturday. Needless to say, it was going to be a rugged week for all the teams.

In his book about Coach Herrin, Matt Wynn (2020) talks about how Coach Herrin wanted to invite six of the best teams from the area. In 1979, Rich's first call was to Bill Chumbler, the head coach at Cairo High School in Cairo, IL (Wynn, 2020). Coach Chumbler agreed to bring the Pilots. Okawville, Pinckneyville, Olney, and Edwardsville were added to Cairo and Benton, and the first year of the new format was set.

In 1982, Coach Herrin called David Lee about having the Foxes replace Edwardsville in the BIT. Coach Lee was a bit hesitant at first because he was not sure we could compete year in and year out as one of the smaller schools in the tournament (Wynn, 2020). In the end, Coach Lee agreed to have the team join the tournament and he said it was one of the best decisions he made while at McLeansboro High School(Wynn, 2020).

Going into the 1984 BIT, we knew it was going to be a challenge for us. We were going to face great programs with coaches that would end up being in the Illinois Basketball Coaches Hall of Fame after they retired. Dave Luectefeld of Okawville, Bill Chumbler of Cairo, Dick Corn at Pinckneyville, and Ron Herrin at Olney. When you add them to Coach Herrin and Coach Lee you have multiple state championships and trips to the state tournament with a lot of hardware coming back to Southern Illinois and over 3500 combined wins.

In 1983, the BIT was loaded with five teams that won twenty games and three teams, McLeansboro, Okawville, and Benton, that made it to the Illinois State Tournament. The 1984 BIT was not quite as strong and I think everyone was thinking if things go as they should, we would be playing Benton on Saturday night with both teams unbeaten for the week and playing for the title. However, we knew we could not look past anyone. Pinckneyville and Cairo both were on their way to having twenty-win seasons and Olney would finish 19-8 that year. Even Okawville, who would finish with under ten wins, could take solace in the fact that their freshman class that year would go on to finish second to Venice High School in 1987.

# 24

# Game 16: Foxes 66 vs Okawville Rockets 46 Foxes 16-0

Our first opponent was the Okawville Rockets. Okawville had an amazing program for a school with under 200 students. They had made it to the state tournament in three of the last four years with a third-place finish in 1980 and losses in the super-sectional in 1982 and 1983. They were in a down year, but they were still very well coached and we could not overlook them.

We jumped out on the Rockets in the first quarter of the game and led 18-10 after the first period. We did not play a great game, but we played well enough to win handily. We led 40-18 at the half and cruised to a 66-46 win. We killed Okawville on the boards by a total of 39-21. Brian has twenty-three points and twenty-one rebounds and nearly out-rebounded Okawville by himself. Tracy had fifteen and Scott and Stacy both pitched in nine points while Bryan Cross finished with eight. We were starting to get more consistent contributions from Stacy, Bryan, and myself. Later in the tournament that would be critical for us to have a chance to win.

Brian hammers a dunk against the Okawville Rockets in the BIT.

Scott Cravens with perfect form on his jumper. Scott was a key "re-addition" to our team in 83-84. Scott was so unselfish and only cared about us winning. He was at times overshadowed by Brian Sloan and Tracy Sturm, but we don't win a state title without his defense throughout the season. Scott "locked up" opponent's best perimeter players every game.

# 25

# Game 17: Foxes 62 Pinckneyville Panthers 41 Foxes 17-0

The Pinckneyville Panthers were our second opponent in the BIT. They had a solid team and were led by one of the top coaches in the state in Dick Corn. Dick was a Benton High School graduate and played for Coach Herrin in the 60s on some of the best Ranger teams in school history. Coach Corn grew up in Macedonia and also had ties to McLeansboro. His mom moved to McLeansboro after his dad got sick and his sister, Jean Ann Winemiller, was an elementary teacher in Hamilton County Unit #10.

This game was tight at the beginning, and we were up 8-6 late in the first quarter and led 13-7 at the end of the first frame. We went on a 19-3 run in the first half and eventually led 28-16 after the second frame. The lead stayed at 12-14 points until early in the fourth quarter when Coach Corn got two technical for arguing with the officials. We shot poorly for the game, but we held the Panthers to under 33% shooting and ended up winning 62-41.

***Dick Corn, Pinckneyville Head Coach:*** *We had four guys on our team who played on Pinckneyville 204 School's state championship team as eighth graders. We just had no answer for your team's size. This team* *was the first group to not win the regional title since I started coaching at PCHS.*

*Coulterville and Coach Rodney Watson beat us in the regional final. Your team should have played them in the Super-sectional, but they celebrated beating us like they won the state title.*

*We simply were no match for you guys. Our kids gave a big effort but just were not skilled enough. I did not get many T's, so I was obviously very frustrated. I was most likely sending a message to our team for the rest of the season. It was very obvious you guys had an exceptional team with players who played for each other and had no egos.*

Once again, Brian led us with twenty points and eleven rebounds. Tracy chipped in fourteen and I finished with twelve for the game. Scott was not feeling great, and Coach Lee rested him a bit more than usual on this night. A key to the win was that we held the Panthers' starting guards, Toby Queen, and Jimmy Carson, to eight points combined.

One thing that happened during the game was Tracy got elbowed in the mouth by Brian on a rebound. Tracy was looking up at the ball as it came down and, as Brian pulled the ball down, his elbow went right into Tracy's mouth. Tracy had to leave the game for a bit to get his tooth put back in place. One of his front teeth was pushed back at almost a ninety-degree angle. He went to the locker room and a dentist went to check on him. They had him bite down on the tongue depressor to put the tooth back in place. I don't think any of us knew how serious it was until after the game. It just showed how tough Tracy was and that rubbed off on all of us. Tracy would have to have a root canal after the tournament was over.

The last game of the night was between Benton and Cairo. We only stayed for a quarter of the game before heading home, but it was obvious that the Pilots had no answer for Bruce Baker. Baker was killing Cairo inside and ended up scoring a career-high forty-three points for the game. I also remember when we were leaving the game to go home, and I looked out on the floor. My dad was officiating the game. I never really thought much about it, but now it seems crazy that my dad was calling games in the same tournament I was playing in for MHS.

We left Rich Herrin Gymnasium after the first quarter and headed home. I think all the players knew that the Rangers we were going to play on Saturday night were a completely different team than the one we faced at SIU Arena in December.

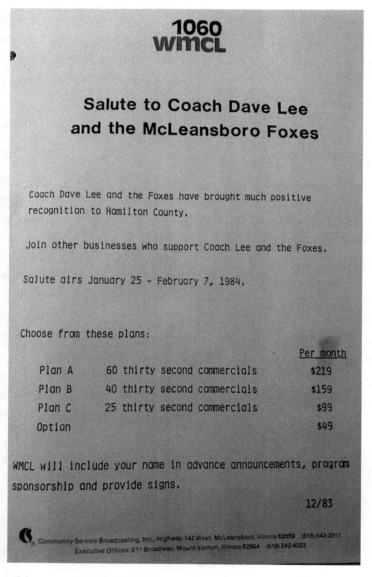

The community in Hamilton County supported our team all season. This was an example of a radio ad offer from WMCL radio during the season.

# 26

# Game 18: Foxes 65 Olney Tigers 44
# Foxes 18-0

Friday night was the start of three games in twenty-four hours for us and our first opponent was the Olney Tigers and Coach Ron Herrin. Olney had another solid team and we were starting three tough games in a short period of time. One thing that happened before the game was, I was not feeling well. I had a fever and was nauseous. I did not tell anyone how bad it was, but I think it was pretty obvious I was not 100%.

Rich Herrin did not do us any favors in the scheduling for the tournament because we played the last game in each of the last three sessions. So, we would get home late on Friday and have to come back for two games on Saturday afternoon and night.

Once again, we methodically dismantled Olney. We led 31-18 at the half and 50-25 after three quarters. For the third game of the tournament, we were able to sub in the fourth and let everyone get some time. We had a really balanced scoring game with Cravens scoring fourteen, Sloan thirteen, Stacy twelve, Cross eleven, Tracy eight, and Ernie Shelton scored a career-high six points in the game.

I remember being happy that we were 3-0 in the tournament, but I was really starting to feel sick. I probably had the flu, but I was not going to the doctor, and I did my best to hide how bad I was feeling. There was no way I would not play on Saturday.

Stacy Sturm goes up for a basket versus the Olney Tigers. Stacy and I played together for three years in high school and parts of two seasons at Rend Lake College. In all my time playing in high school and college, Stacy was the best post player I ever teamed up with. He made my job as a passer easy.

# 27

# Game 19: Foxes 70 Cairo Pilots 58
# Foxes 19-0

When I was a young kid, Cairo was always one of my favorite teams to watch play. I believe that for most fans, the only time you rooted against Cairo was when they played your team. Cairo, IL is a very small town on the farthest tip of Southern Illinois where the Ohio and Mississippi rivers connect.

Coach Chumbler took the job at Cairo in the early 70s at a time when there was a lot of racial unrest across the nation. Cairo was a school of almost all African American students and their basketball teams did not have many White players on the team. Most schools would not schedule Cairo and their program was not very good (Wynn, 2020). When Coach Chumbler was hired, he started going to the local park and playing with the Cairo kids (Wynn, 2020).

Bill was a standout player at Murray State and could still keep up with the kids he was playing against. They figured out really quickly that Coach Chumbler could ball, and he ended up having fifty-six kids try out for the team that first year. Cairo quickly became one of the top programs in the state.

The two things I loved about the Pilots were, first, they dunked before and during the games. That was not very common back then. The second thing I remember is that they had some great names on their roster. Guys like Verandes Kinnard, Taurice Mallory, Armone Mathews, Selma Snow, and Lorenzo Duncan.

I also had the good fortune to play with former Pilots, Armone Mathews and Michael Ayers, at Rend Lake College. I know that I can speak for the other Foxes on the team that we loved playing with those guys.

Leading up to the game we talked about how to attack Cairo. The previous year the Foxes played them three times. Cairo won the first two games in tight battles, but they never pressed us. In the third game in the sectional finals, Cairo pressed and McLeansboro attacked them for the entire game. McLeansboro beat Cairo in a blowout by a score of 89-66.

When we got on the bus to head to Benton, I was feeling much worse. I did everything I could to not let anyone know how bad I felt. Brian knew I was sick, and he told me that Coach Smithpeters asked if he thought I could go. Brian said, "I know Jeff wants to play awfully bad."

When we got about five miles outside of Benton, we noticed that there was a lot of graffiti on signs and billboards. The Benton fans had painted 'Foxes will be 19-1' and lots of other phrases that are not appropriate for this book. I think we all thought it was kind of funny.

Cairo had no returning starters from the previous year's 28-3 team, but they still had a lot of talent and a really good guard in junior, Shawn Box. Cairo came out and pressed us again. We did not have time to practice against their pressure, but we really did not need to at this point in the season. One of the misnomers about our team was that we played a slowdown game. That could not have been further from the truth. We played a patient and smart offensive game, but if you pressed us, we were going to try to get layups. If we did not get layups, we would make you guard us versus our half-court offense.

One other sidenote that some of the players noticed was Coach Lee was wearing this Kelly-Green sport coat. He had worn the same coat when we played Eldorado in the semifinals and in the title game against Harrisburg, he wore a green and white plaid jacket. I am sure most people thought they were not too appealing, but the Foxes' fans loved it.

Stacy Sturm and I wondered aloud if Coach Lee would wear the plaid jacket for the game against Benton that night...which he did.

We carried out our game plan really well and jumped out to a 22-12 lead after a quarter. The halftime score was 36-21 and we cruised to a 70-58 win. Brian came up huge for us again with 24 points and 17 rebounds while Tracy chipped in with 22 and Stacy had 12. It was a good win for us leading into the game against Benton.

# 28

# *Before the Rematch*

After the game, we went to a hotel on the east side of Benton to rest and eat before the final. I was rooming with Tracy, and I felt absolutely awful. In all honesty, I should not have played. One, because I had not eaten in two days and also because I was not sure I was going to be helping our team. I almost went to Coach Lee and told him to start Crossy.

The team and cheerleaders went across the street to eat supper. I really wanted to stay in the room and sleep, but I was convinced to try to eat. Everyone was eating and I felt like I was going to throw up. Sue Easton, our cheerleading sponsor, brought me a bowl of soup and I took about three bites. I really should have taken an IV to get hydrated, but that was not something that was done back then.

After dinner, we went back to the room. After about fifteen minutes, I jumped up and went to the bathroom. I threw up all over the bathtub and toilet. I was sure I was dying. I don't know if Coach Lee was thinking about having me on the bench to start the game because he never said anything to me. Actually, the best thing for me was to play and get my body temperature up because I did feel a bit better during the games. It was when I cooled off that I felt the worst.

At about 9:00 p.m., we headed to Rich Herrin gymnasium for a rematch with the Rangers. We were 19-0 and they were 14-5, but they were playing really well and not even close to the team we played earlier in the season. This was going to be a great battle between two great teams.

# 29

# Game 20: Foxes 48 Benton Rangers 45
# Foxes 20-0

Rich Herrin Gymnasium is one of the most iconic gyms in Southern Illinois. Benton high school had about 700 students in 1984, but the gym's capacity is about 4000 or so. On this night, I am pretty sure the fire marshal either stayed home or turned a blind eye because there had to be 5000 people in the gym. There were people sitting everywhere. The lobbies were standing-room only. My mom had to sit in the aisle on the steps at the top of the gym.

> **Ron Smith, Benton Rangers' Asst. Coach:** *The game we played you guys at SIU had a great crowd, but the game in the final of the BIT was the biggest crowd I have ever seen at Rich Herrin Gymnasium.*

This game was like a heavyweight fight with both teams playing very conservatively and probing each other for weaknesses. The game was tied at 9-9 after the first quarter and we led 20-19 at the half.

We went in at halftime feeling ok, but knowing we had to find a way to solve Benton's defense. I was also concerned about how I was feeling. During the games, I felt all right because my body temperature would go up and I would sweat. It was when I stopped and cooled down that I felt terrible again. We were in the locker room and waiting for Coach Lee to come talk to us about the second half of the game. I was sitting in a chair without a warmup jacket on and I was shivering. Right then, Tony Rubenacker came over and put his warmup on me. Again, just another example of the kinds of guys we had on our team.

Benton was playing a triangle and two. They played man-to-man on Brian and Tracy and had a 1-2 zone in the lane. Scott and I were out front, and we needed one of us to step up. I felt confident that I could make shots when needed, but it was not going to happen tonight. Scott and I would finish the game 5-18 from the floor combined. Brian did not score a field goal until the fourth quarter and Tracy scored two points for the game.

**Don Lewis:** *During the game, Brian had a hard time holding on to the ball. Coach Lee came over to me and told me every time out, give Brian the rosin. The first time out came, and I gave Brian the rosin. Brian was frustrated and he threw it on the floor and under the bleachers. Of course, Coach Lee immediately asked me, "Where's the rosin?" and I was in a panic trying to find it.*

Tracy also had to guard Bruce Baker for most of the game. Bruce was 6'7 and 205 lbs. while Tracy was 6'1 and 170. Tracy battled Bruce all night long, but Bruce was the best player on the floor for most of the game. Bryan Cross led us with eight points at the half and he was the main reason we were still in the game.

Benton went on a 12-2 run to start the third quarter and led 31-22. I remember the Benton fans were going crazy and I could not hear anything. Coach Lee put Crossy in the game and moved Scott to the baseline. We ran an offense called 'Spot 2' with Crossy and me on the top against one defender and the other three guys on the baseline cutting and screening to get open. We just could not solve their defense because I could not make anything. We made a run at the end of the third to cut the lead to three. Cross hit a jumper and Brian and Tracy made a couple of free throws. We were down 33-30 with one quarter left.

We went on an 8-2 run to start the quarter to go up 38-35. Cross and Cravens both hit big jumpers for us. Benton led 39-38 with a few minutes left in the game when the legend of 'The Phantom' was born. Bryan Cross hit three straight jumpers from the left elbow and we gained a lead of five points that we would not relinquish.

Brian hit two free throws with nine seconds left and us leading 46-45. The final score was 48-45 and was one of the best High School games I was ever involved in. Bruce Baker played a tremendous game with Tracy all over him for thirty-two minutes. Baker finished with twenty-nine points and eight rebounds.

*Bryan Cross: I get asked about the game against Benton in the 1984 BIT all the time and, of course, I am always happy to talk about it (Wynn, 2020).*

For the first time in a while, we played only six guys. Brian had ten points and six boards, Cravens had seven points, I chipped in with five and Stacy Sturm finished with four points. The star of the game was Bryan Cross or 'The Phantom' as he would soon be called later in the year. Crossy scored twenty points on 8-10 shooting from the floor and 4-4 on free throws. Every basket he made was from 15-18 feet.

I don't know where Crossy's nickname, 'The Phantom', came from. I am fairly certain Mark Snyder, Heath Lasswell, or Ernie Shelton started it. In all the years I played with Bryan at MHS and Rend Lake College, I never heard him say more than five words in one conversation. The rest of the year we ran a lot of sets for Bryan, and he shot 70% from the floor. I would estimate that he might have made two layups all year.

*Ron Smith, Benton Rangers' Assistant Coach: The last thing I remember about the games against McLeansboro that season is how much I hated hearing their fans sing Put Another Log on the Fire. It made me think of 'it's not over till the fat lady sings' or way back in the NBA when Red Auerbach, the coach of the Boston Celtics in the 1960s, used to light up a cigar on the bench when he knew his team was going to win.*

We really celebrated this victory. Benton had a great team and would go on to represent the South in the AA State Tourney at the end of the year. I remember feeling great about our win, but also feeling bad for Coach Herrin and his players. From 1983-1985, Benton was 12-0 against everyone else at the tournament and 0-3 against us. They lost three nailbiters to finish 4-1 each year. In 1983, the Foxes won 66-63 in OT and in 1985, we beat Benton 39-38 in 2OT. I am fairly certain those are tough losses for those guys to think about, but they were great teams and were always classy. We had a lot of respect for them.

The celebration continued back home in McLeansboro for everyone but me. The team met at Auten's Pizza with what seemed like 500 fans waiting for us inside and outside the building. I stopped by for a second and Coach Lee told me to go home and get some rest. I did not argue. We were now 20-0 and ready for the last seven games of the regular season.

I contacted several former Rangers players who were on the floor that night for their memories of our games that season. Guys like Randy House, Kai Nurnberger, Daren Carlisle, and Bruce Baker. I was not able to get any of them to contribute to this book and I think I respected them even more for not responding. In all honesty, if the roles had been reversed and one of them contacted me to talk about them beating us twice and winning a state title, I don't think I would have given them anything. Those feelings between our teams run deep.

*Jim Melton, Foxes' Reserve Guard: One of my favorite memories—I've told this story many times over the years—is the road signs on the Saturday of Benton tourney. They were spray painted 'Foxes suck' or 'Foxes 19-1' etc. all the way from the county line to Benton. Then they were on fire on the way home!*

*Chris Aaron, Benton High School Class of 1986: I was certainly looking forward to the Benton-McLeansboro game at the BIT in 1984, especially since the Foxes had beaten us 66-63 the year before. Student attendance at the games was very strong when I was in school and many of us attended every game of every session of the Invitational-both to root for the Rangers and heckle the other teams. I distinctly recall making fun of Bryan Cross' uniform all week, because the numbers on the back of both the green and white sets were small and faded.*

*As the week wore on, it was apparent the Rangers and Foxes were on a collision course, and most likely both would be 4-0 heading into Saturday night. Sure enough, that's what happened. Following the afternoon session on Saturday, we went to grab something to eat and hustled back to the gym. There were people, lots of people, probably a thousand or more standing outside the gym when we got there.*

*In fairly short order the doors opened, and we rushed in. It seemed like the gym was full within about fifteen minutes of the doors opening. The first two games were just something to be endured while we waited for the main event. More and more people kept coming in, standing, and sitting in every available space in Rich Herrin Gym. Easily the most people I have ever seen in a High School gym. The Rangers and Foxes took the floor for warmups, and I thought the roof might blow off of the place, both from the roar of the crowd and the fact it was hotter than hell in there.*

*As far as the game itself, my main recollection is Bryan Cross (he and the faded little uniform numbers) absolutely shooting the lights out. The game was tense, but I knew we were going to eventually pull it out for a measure of revenge for '83 and the Tip-Off Classic, but the Foxes prevailed 48-45. No way could we have lost to the Foxes again (they were from McLeansboro, for God's sake-we thought they were all farmers and bumpkins). Other than a numb feeling after losing to the Foxes (again), I don't remember much about the postgame. I was just ready to get my fifteen-year-old self out of there, so I didn't have to watch them celebrate on our floor, again.*

*Looking back on it now, I realize how fortunate we all (players and fans) were to have been involved in something like that. Huge crowd, tight game, future D-1 players, and Mr. Basketball, an eventual Class A state champ in McLeansboro and a Benton squad who knocked off undefeated Carbondale in the sectional on their way to an Elite Eight appearance at the Big House. That Saturday night was simply something incredible to see.*

**Holly Sloan:** *The BIT Championship…or what we like to call 'The Phantom Game.' As unassuming as Bryan Cross was, Benton was completely focused on containing Brian and Tracy. Crossy stood at the elbow all night and hit shot after shot. They had no answer for him."*

BIT Champs!!!! All I was thinking about after the win was going home and throwing up.

Brian Sloan goes up for a jumper over Benton's Jay Schaefer (35) in the final game of the 1984 BIT. The Foxes would win a "barn burner" 48-45 in front of some 5000 fans at Rich Herrin Gym.

Brian posting up against Daren Carlisle in the final game of the BIT. Benton played a triangle-and-two the entire game and led by nine in the middle of the 3rd period. Thankfully, Bryan Cross saved us with twenty points off the bench that night.

Brian Sloan and Bryan Cross go up for a rebound against the Benton Rangers.
We dominated teams on the glass all season and were seldom outrebounded
because of Brian, Crossy and Stacy Sturm.

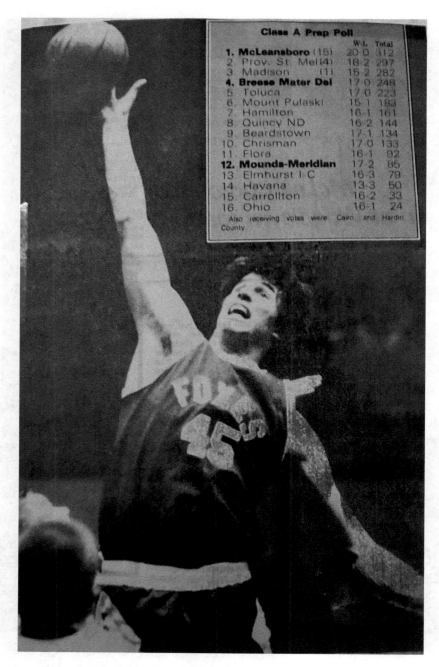

| Class A Prep Poll | | |
|---|---|---|
| | W-L | Total |
| **1. McLeansboro** (15) | 20-0 | 312 |
| 2. Prov. St. Mel (4) | 18-2 | 297 |
| 3. Madison (1) | 15-2 | 282 |
| **4. Breese Mater Dei** | 17-0 | 248 |
| 5. Toluca | 17-0 | 223 |
| 6. Mount Pulaski | 15-1 | 183 |
| 7. Hamilton | 16-1 | 161 |
| 8. Quincy ND | 16-2 | 144 |
| 9. Beardstown | 17-1 | 134 |
| 10. Chrisman | 17-0 | 133 |
| 11. Flora | 16-1 | 92 |
| **12. Mounds-Meridian** | 17-2 | 85 |
| 13. Elmhurst I C | 16-3 | 79 |
| 14. Havana | 13-3 | 50 |
| 15. Carrollton | 16-2 | 33 |
| 16. Ohio | 16-1 | 24 |

Also receiving votes were Cairo, and Hardin County

Brian Sloan with one of his many blocked or changed shots from the season. The graphic shows one of the first times we were ranked #1 in class A in the Illinois.

Bryan Cross goes up for two of his twenty points he scored against Benton in the final game of the 1984 BIT. "The Phantom" saved our season. We trailed 31-22 in the middle of the 3rd quarter and things looked bad for us. Crossy was 8-10 from the floor and 4-4 from the line with 12 points in the final eleven minutes of the game and clinched out BIT Title.

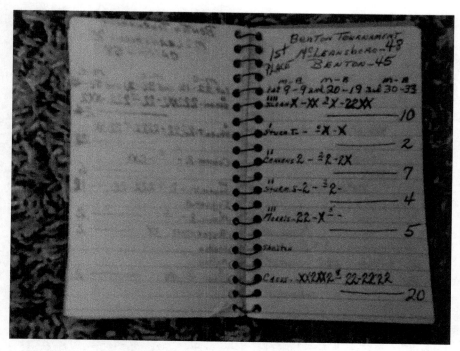

Dick Auten, long time Fox fan, kept his own "scorebook" of McLeansboro/Hamilton County boys' basketball game from 1970-2019. Dick had a notebook for each season. This is the box score Dick kept from the BIT game when the Foxes beat Benton 48-45 to win the BIT title.

# Foxes 'Cross' Up Benton Strategy To Win Tourney

The headline after our win and Bryan Cross' performance after we beat Benton to win the BIT.

The 83-84 Benton Rangers played two great games against us in 83-84. They would go on to finish 24-7 and make the Elite Eight at State.

# 30

## Game 21: Foxes 87 Fairfield Mules 45
## Foxes 21-0

Once again, we hit the road for a game against Fairfield. If anyone was thinking we were going to have a letdown after winning the BIT, they were mistaken. Earlier, I said that there were three games that I thought we played about as close to perfect as we could. This was the second of those games. Some people call it 'getting into the zone.' Well, we got in a zone on this night.

This game was over by the end of the first quarter. I think we were still ticked about the Mules scoring sixty points on us the first time we played, and we wanted to send a message to them that we were better than that now.

We came out and pressured Fairfield all of the floor with our 1-2-2 press and half-court defense. We led 21-8 after the first quarter and 49-19 at the half. We did not miss a shot from the field in the second quarter of the game. Brian played one of his best games with seventeen points and ten boards along with several great passes. Brian also had a monster dunk in the game on a play set up by Coach Lee. The thing I loved about Coach Lee was, even though he was hard-nosed as anyone I have ever known, he liked to have fun too. There were a few times when our teams were up big that he would set up something for someone to get a dunk. I think he knew that we had to put up with a lot from him and the other coaches and it was kind of a reward for us and the fans.

Once again, we cruised to a good win and played one of our best games of the season. The final score was 87-45 and we shot a blistering 75.6% from the floor for the game. Brian, Tracy, Stacy, and Scott all scored in double figures and the subs played the entire fourth quarter.

When the next AP poll came out, we were the unanimous #1 team in Class A in Illinois. I don't think any of us thought much about our ranking. We knew we had to compete every second to beat teams. I am certain Coach Lee would agree that he had a bunch of really good kids at MHS. Not just our team, but the guys before us like Darin Lee, Curtie Reed, Kevin Kirsch, the late Rod Irvin, and Brad Lee. David did not have to worry about us doing anything to embarrass ourselves or the team. We were all really good students and, overall, pretty good kids. Being the unanimous #1 in the state was not going to change our approach to the season because we had six games left before we started postseason play.

After the Fairfield game, we had ten days off before facing Christopher on the following Friday. On Monday, we came to practice and Darin Lee, Coach Lee's son, brought some of the RLC guys over to scrimmage against us. Former Cairo Pilots, Michael Ayers, and Armone Mathews came over every day that week and scrimmaged us with Darin and a few other guys. They were all redshirting that year, so Coach had asked RLC's coach, Mitch Haskins, if we could borrow them for a few days because we were not preparing for Christopher on Friday or Nashville on Saturday. We spent the week getting ready for Evansville Bosse and their vaunted press.

Before practice started, Coach Lee called me over and told me he was going to start giving Bryan Cross more minutes. I understood it, but I did not like it. He said that I was going to start on the side during practice. For four days I sat on the sideline and watched us scrimmage. I thought I would get in some, but Coach Lee did not put me in any of the scrimmages that week.

I was really down. I knew I had to be ready and that I had to be unselfish because Crossy had earned more minutes. I felt like I had to do something to get some shots in, so every night that week after dinner I went back to the gym. I just worked on my game like it was the summertime. I did not tell anybody in my family that I was not going to be starting on Friday because I was pretty embarrassed. But I knew I had to do what was best for the team.

One other thing that happened was that there was a rumor going around that Coach Lee was trying get one of our later opponents to drop their game with us so that we could play the Carbondale Terriers at SIU Arena. Carbondale was also undefeated and ranked high in Class AA. Coach had allegedly approached Tom Wheeler, coach of our next opponent, about dropping us. That never came to fruition and in later years I asked both Coach Lee and Wheels if it was true. They both denied it, but I still believe that sounds like something Coach Lee would have at least considered.

Foxes fans showed their support through all kinds of weather.

# 31

## *Practice at the Sturm's Gym*

One of the things that Coach Lee did throughout the season was try to create interest in our team in areas outside of Hamilton County. David did a tremendous job of building excitement and creating support from people all over Southern Illinois.

We had some time off after the Fairfield game. Coach Lee decided to have us practice at Tracy and Stacy Sturm's house on a Thursday after school was dismissed.

Tracy and Stacy lived about twenty minutes southwest of McLeansboro near Macedonia. Their parents, Tom and Carolyn, had turned the old, Flanagan School into their home. I spent many hours with Stacy at their property riding four-wheelers. The Sturms had left the gym pretty much as it was. It had the old tile floor with no bleachers and one end of the court had the rim and backboard in place. Tracy and Stacy could go shoot and play one-on-one anytime they liked.

Coach Lee decided to give us a 'day off and all the players and coaches drove to the Sturm's house for a light practice. Members of the local press were invited to come and watch us as we shot around for about an hour or so. It was a brilliant move on David's part because it was just another unique and interesting story for people to read about our team.

**Heath Lasswell:** *Every memory from that season is a favorite of mine, but the practice at Tracy and Stacy Sturm's house stands out simply because we had been working so hard and focusing so much on the season. Practicing at a different place for that evening was fun and sort of relaxing.*

**David Lee:** *There was a unique practice at the Sturm boys' house. An AP sportswriter asked me if it was true that the Sturms had a gym in their home. I told him it was, and we might have a practice session there and I would invite him. I also invited the local TV stations. In the back of my mind, I really wanted to see it since I had graduated from eighth grade there when it was a school. The Sturms had bought the school and turned it into their home.*

**Derek Harlan, Mt. Vernon HIGH SCHOOL Class of 1993, and my stepbrother:** *My dad was friends with the Sturm's dad. One Sunday after the season was over, Dad took me to their house to shoot around in their gym. When we got there, not only were Tracy and Stacy there, but so was Brian Sloan! I felt like I was hanging out with the Beatles! Of all my memories from that season, that one is probably my favorite. All those guys were so nice to me and to this day I have never forgotten it.*

Tom Sturm with his son's, Tracy and Stacy, in the gym at their home southwest of McLeansboro. Tom and his wife, Carolyn, bought the old Flanagan school and turned it into their home. Tracy and Stacy had a gym to play in any time they wanted.

## 32

## Game 22: Foxes 66 Christopher 46
## Foxes 22-0

Normally, leading up to a game, we would spend the time in practice preparing for the next opponent. However, Coach Lee said he learned a hard lesson the previous year by not looking ahead to teams that we might play later in the year. David felt like he should have prepared for Flanagan in the 1983 state semifinal sooner than he did and it cost the team a 39-34 loss.

In the ten days or so leading up to the weekend before the Bosse game, we did not spend any time talking about or preparing for our rematch with Christopher (sorry Coach Wheeler) or Nashville the next night. We talked about Christopher during our walk-through at the end of school on Friday. I went home and prepared myself to be the sixth man. My main worry was my mom going off on Coach Lee when she saw I was on the bench.

We were in the locker room before the game getting dressed and ready for our typical pregame talk about our opponent. I fully expected Crossy to start in my place. Coach Lee put the starters' names on the board, and they were Sloan, T. Sturm, Cravens, Cross, and....Morris. I am not sure who was more shocked...Stacy Sturm or me. All week I had not practiced at all, and Coach Lee put me in the starting lineup over Stacy. To this day, I have no idea why Coach did that.

The game at Christopher started out like many of the other games we played that year. We jumped out early and did not let up. We were up 36-23 at the half. Once again, Brian got his fourth foul in the third quarter and had to go to the bench. Christopher came back and made things interesting by cutting the lead to four points. Coach Lee put Brian back in the game and he fed the ball to Stacy for three straight field goals, and we blew the game open to lead 55-32 after the third period. This was another fourth quarter where our bench players got on the floor. Brian was dominant with twenty-four points and eleven rebounds, Stacy had his best game up to that point with eighteen, and Cravens finished with twelve.

I have to give Stacy credit because he did not let starting on the bench affect him at all and had one of his best games of the season. This was just another example of how unselfish our players were. Stacy could have been upset about not starting, but he went out and had one of his best games.

Stacy Sturm goes up for two against the Christopher Bearcats. Stacy came off the bench for the first time this game and never said a word. Everyone on our team cared about one thing.....WINNING!!

# 33

# Game 23: Foxes 67 Nashville Hornets 48
# Foxes 23-0

This was our first home game in over a month and MHS gym was rockin'. The game was 'standing-room-only.' We even had the bleachers on the stage pulled out and young kids were sitting on the stage with their feet hanging over the edge.

A funny thing happened that night before the game. We finished our pregame in the locker room and were standing on the steps leading up to the floor preparing to go warm up. That was a really exciting part of our games because the gym was always loud and the band would play the Notre Dame Fighting Irish fight song, our school song, as we came out.

A few minutes before we ran on the floor, Tony Rubenacker very dryly said, "Could you guys not blow these guys out tonight? I don't really feel like playing in this game."

We all cracked up...oh, and we made sure Tony ended up having to play.

The game against Nashville was a special night for us. Coach Lee and our team were not much about individual accolades. Coach Lee, Coach Reed, Coach Smithpeters, and Jerry Sloan preached to us the importance of the team first. On this night, Brian, and Tracy both scored their 1000th point for their careers.

Coach Lee also had led the program to our 100th win in just over three and a half seasons. In fact, in the five seasons from 1980-1985, our record was 137-20 with a state title and a third-place finish. That five-year run was even more impressive considering we played really strong competition. Coach Lee always seemed to have the attitude that we would play 'anyone, anywhere, anytime' because that would make us better at the end of the season.

Nashville had a really solid program, and we came out a little flat against the Hornets. They were not as strong as they had been in previous years, but they had a great tradition and were well-coached. In fact, they were the last team from Southern Illinois to win a state title when they won it all in 1978. Also, Coach Lee's son, Darin, would go on to coach at Nashville from 1992-2009 and win over 400 games there.

The score at the end of the first quarter was tied, 14-14. In the second quarter, we took control and led 35-20 at the half. In the third quarter, we picked up where we left off before the half and led 53-33. Tracy led us with nineteen points and even had a dunk in the third quarter. Brian had sixteen, Scott pitched in with twelve and Stacy Sturm had another strong game with ten points.

We were now 23-0 and ready to head to Evansville to play at Robert's Stadium and face our next opponent...the Bosse Bulldogs.

Coach Lee helping the officials with a call during a game. Coach did not have to say much to the officials during the season.

# 34

# Leading Up to the Bosse Game

I am not sure there were many High School games that had the hype leading up to our game against Bosse in 1984. I am certain Coach Lee got them on the schedule to prepare us for really good teams in the post-season and specifically, Chicago Providence St. Mel.

Bosse had one of the top programs in Indiana. The previous two years they had finished the regular season undefeated. I had watched them play in the semifinals of the Indiana State Finals in 1982 against Gary Roosevelt. Bosse had one of the best players in the nation in Derrick Dowell. Bosse lost that game to Roosevelt 58-57. Roosevelt's best player was Renaldo Thomas, who would go on to play at the University of Houston with Hakeem Olajuwon, Clyde Drexler, and Phi Slamma Jamma. Dowell went on to play at USC and had an outstanding college career. He likely would have played in the NBA, but he tore his Achilles and was never the same.

Coach Lee used this game to really build support for us from all over Southern Illinois. This game was not McLeansboro vs. Bosse. It was a small school from Southern Illinois against the big school from Evansville, Indiana. Bosse's team was not quite as strong as the previous two years, but they were still really good. Their best player, Evie Waddell, had been a starter for three years and was an outstanding player.

***David Lee:*** *One of the big games during the season was with Bosse High School in Evansville, Indiana. I scheduled Bosse to play at Roberts Stadium in order for the players, especially Brian, to play where Jerry played in college and where I had played several games. I knew that the atmosphere at Roberts Stadium would prepare us for any team in Illinois, including the State tournament.*

The Sunday edition of the Evansville Courier came out with a full-page write-up about the game. The writers for the Southern Illinois High School basketball and Southern Indiana High School basketball wrote 'letters' to each other explaining why their side would win. The premise for both was about size. We had a significant size advantage over Bosse, but they were a school about four times our size. It made for a great story.

There were also other connections between Evansville and our program. Brian's dad, Jerry, was perhaps the greatest player in the history of the Evansville Aces. There were all kinds of pictures in the Robert's Stadium trophy case of Jerry playing at U of E. Jerry was almost as beloved in Evansville as he was in McLeansboro. Jerry's senior year the Aces won the college division title by beating his best friend, David Lee, and the SIU Salukis.

I also had a connection with the Evansville Aces, but it was a bit more tragic. Mike Duff and Kevin Kingston, whom I knew from my dad's time at Eldorado High School, were playing for the Aces in 1977. I knew Kevin and his family and Mike was my first basketball hero. On December 13, 1977, the Aces were flying to play Middle Tennessee State. It was a very cold, icy night and the plane crashed soon after take-off. Everyone on board was killed. It was one of the worst nights of my young life to that point.

# This one is more than just another game

Dear Jay:

"Put another log on the fire."

You'll hear that country song plenty Tuesday night, when McLeansboro's Foxes come into Roberts Stadium to crash Bosse.

Eddie Allen, a radio color man, sings that tune every time the Foxes are sure of victory. It's the McLeansboro answer to Don Meredith's "Turn out the lights, the party's over." Like Red Auerbach lighting up a cigar whenever his Celtics were beyond reach.

Allen has sung 23 times this winter, each time the Foxes have played. He'll make a 24th rendition Tuesday, reminding Bosse fans of the Valentine's Day Massacre. The Bulldogs will meet their match in 6-foot-8 Brian Sloan and the rest of David Lee's superbly coached Foxes.

Oh, Bosse's quickness may pose a few early problems. But the Foxes proved they can handle quickness when they drubbed Cairo Senior by 20 points in last year's Illinois Class A sectional finals, en route to a third-in-the-state finish. Sloan and Tracy Sturm, a guard who favorably impressed then University of Evansville assistant Richard Skaggs, are back from that unit and their new teammates play roles to the hilt.

Like his father Jerry Sloan, young Brian plays with intensity rarely seen on high school courts. Bosse has nobody to guard him. Nor have the Bulldogs faced a shot-blocker like the latest addition to Bobby Knight U.

Again like his father, Sloan is a three-dimensional player. He rebounds (13 per game) and plays defense. So do all the Foxes. Gen. Lee played at Southern Illinois, where he learned Jack Hartman's defensive schemes so well he was voted the school's Athlete Of The Year in 1966. Like Indiana, McLeansboro plays a helping man-to-man that cuts off easy baskets. And the Foxes block out on their defensive board.

They are not a one-man team. Sloan (19.5 points per game) is joined in double figures by Tracy Sturm (15) and Scott Cravens (12), a defensive stopper. Stacy Sturm, Tracy's brother, averages eight points as a sophomore, while Jeff Morris can score far more than his 5.5 average if necessary. Du Quoin defied Morris to shoot and he shot in 24 points.

Benton held Sloan to 10 points with triple-coverage a while back. So Bryan Morris came off the bench to score 20. Another log on the fire.

The Foxes probably couldn't beat Illinois' best Class AA teams. But Indiana isn't Illinois. Illinois coaches watching Evansville-Terre Haute semistates in recent years say Hoosier shooting just isn't what it's said to be.

The natives may say, Jay, that Illinois should have more players because Illinois is bigger. They're right. There's nothing one can do about its bigness. Come 10 p.m. Tuesday, nothing to do but watch the fire glow.

Happy Valentine's Day.

*Pete Swanson*
Illinois prep editor

---

Dear Pete:

If you've set aside a good book at home to read, Tuesday may be perfect for it.

Sure, there's going to be quite a basketball game at Roberts Stadium, but as a native Illinoisan, you'll probably want to avoid it.

It's the opening night of fox hunting season in Southern Indiana, you know, by declaration of a pack of Bosse Bulldogs.

It's not that McLeansboro isn't good. The Foxes are sly, worthy, top-ranked and undefeated. All that good stuff. They're not going to be nearly quick enough though.

After running up and down the 10 extra feet of the collegiate-length floor, it won't be long before McLeansboro is painfully aware that Bosse's speed is like nothing they've seen all season.

"Big games" like Tuesday's aren't new to Bosse. The Bulldogs have had so many of them in winning 83 of 92 games since Joe Mullan took over. They're 16-3 with 15 straight victories this season.

Agreed, it won't be easy containing Indiana University-bound Brian Sloan, but McLeansboro doesn't have a soul who can stop Bulldog guard Mark Freels (18.8 ppg) from at least matching Sloan's offensive output. He had a career-high 31 points against Tell City last week.

Another senior, Evie Wadde... ...g's leading rebounder. His 13.6 scoring average may not seem like much, but he's reached double figures in all but three games. Forwards Barry (7.9 ppg) and Chris Johnson (7.4 ppg) aren't offensive wizards, either, but they've scored in double figures consistently lately.

If the Foxes turn their attention from guard Robert Calhoun and his 6.2 average, they'll see how he scored 31 points in the final two games of last year's sectional tournament.

Bosse won't make the mistake of assuming that McLeansboro is a one-man team. Mullan knows any one of six Foxes can score, so no box-and-one's or diamond-and-two's are planned for Sloan. The Bulldogs will front him defensively and seek weak-side help.

No doubt Sloan's a good one and you say he's a nice kid, too, huh? But come Wednesday morning, Brian's dad, Jerry, will still be the only Sloan to experience victory at Roberts Stadium.

The natives may say, Pete, that Bosse should win because it has more talent to choose from with a huge enrollment edge (1,142-456). They're right. There's nothing one can do about its bigness.

Come 9 p.m. Tuesday, the Foxes will have slowed to a trot and more than a few Illinoisans burned themselves attempting to drop another log on the fire.

Happy Valentine's Day.

*Jay Stockman*
Indiana prep editor

Before the Bosse game, the Illinois and Indiana prep editors wrote letters to each other explaining why each team would win.

This was in the Evansville-Courier before we played Bosse. Needless to say, this was not "just another high school basketball game."

# 35

# *The History of 'The Log'*

When we ran on the floor before the Bosse game, we had a new addition to our team...a log. Eddie Allen, one of our radio announcers' had started a tradition of singing a version of the song "Put Another Log on the Fire" when it was clear we were going to win a game. The original song was written by American writer and poet, Shel Silverstein, and performed by Tompall Glaser and a few others. Eddie Allen changed the lyrics for the version he sang at the end of our wins to:

> *Put Another Log on the Fire (Foxes version)*
> *Put another log on the fire,*
> *cook me up some bacon and some beans.*
> *Put another win in the column Mom,*
> *we are as happy as can be.*
> *Wash my shirt and iron my green silk britches.*
> *Hang them up as neatly as can be.*
> *Put another log on the fire,*
> *We are coming home with another victory.*

Before we ran out on the floor, Mark Auten was standing in front of us with a log held above his head. Mark led us out and we ran onto the floor to warm up. Mark did this every game the rest of the season up until the state tournament. The log was painted Kelly Green and had our record (23-0) painted on it.

**Mark Auten, MHS Class of 82:** *Before the game against the Bosse Bulldogs and the Foxes, I decided to bring a log as a way to liven up the crowd…and the log began. After the thrilling one-point victory over one of the top teams in Indiana, destiny was staring us squarely in the face. I took the log and gave it numerous coats of Kelly-Green spray paint and made stencils to place on the log to change the number for the win total before the next game. Every game through the super-sectional, I would lead the team out on the floor, with the log over my head. When we got to Champaign, they would not let me bring the log into the Assembly Hall. Fortunately, I was able to contact the cheerleaders and they were able to get it into the Assembly Hall. I proudly held it up in front of the massive 'Green Wave.'*

*The trip back from Champaign involved numerous times climbing through a sunroof to hoist the log. The final trip for 'The Log' was to one final time lead the team into a completely packed Foxes Den at the old MHS gym. The log sat in the trophy case with State tournament trophies for several years until it finally succumbed to decay and had to be put to rest.*

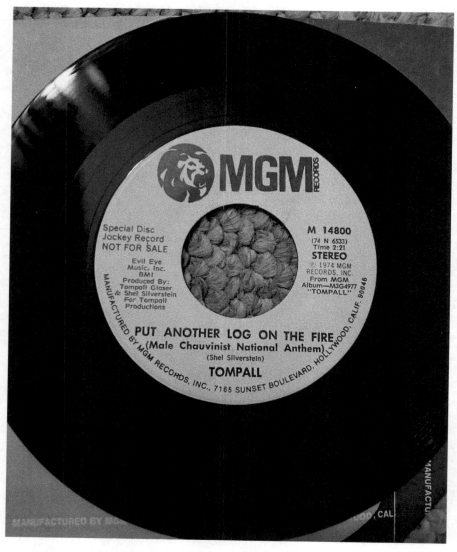

A 45rpm record of the original "Put Another Log on the Fire" song. I doubt many people knew that it was also called the "Make Chauvinist's National Anthem."

Another log

The first game the "log" led us out on the floor being carried by Mark Auten.
Teams hated that song and tried in vein to prevent our fans from
singing it after a win in 83-84.

# 36

# Game 24: Foxes 48 Bosse Bulldogs 47
# Foxes 24-0

Since this game was on a Tuesday and we had to drive over an hour from McLeansboro to Evansville, Indiana, we did something we only did once in my entire time playing for Coach Lee. We had a pregame meal as a team at the old Cupboard Restaurant. I remember that place having a giant chicken on the roof that kids used to mess with all the time or try to steal and also having pretty good food.

The game against Bosse was played at Robert's Stadium home of the Evansville Aces. There were somewhere around 8,000 people at the game. Not only was the crowd big, but the game was going to be televised on tape delay. WFIE Channel 14 in Evansville was going to have the game on their station after the 10:00 p.m. news. This was going to be quite an event.

Bosse was led by longtime coach, Joe Mullan. Besides their senior forward, 6'3 Evie Waddell, the Bulldogs had some other talented players. Mark Freels, a senior guard, was their second leading scorer and Robert Calhoun was their 5'10 junior point guard who was jet quick. Bosse was known for a suffocating press and man-to-man half-court defense. We knew we were going to have to play really well to have a chance to win.

This game lived up to all the hype and then some. Bosse came out and jumped to an early 13-6 lead. It was the only time all year we trailed by more than four points. At the start of the game, Tracy was guarding the 5'10 Calhoun, who was very quick. Scott was guarding Freels, who was about four inches taller than Cravens. Coach Lee had Scott and Tracy switch whom they were guarding, and it proved to be a pivotal adjustment in the game. Evie Waddell was listed as a forward, but he handled the ball outside a lot. Brian was assigned to guard him and worked his tail off the entire game. Waddell hit multiple shots from 20-25 feet early in the game and Brian was all over him. We made a run in the last part of the first quarter to cut the Bosse lead to 17-15. Bosse led for most of the game, but we stayed within a couple of baskets to remain within striking distance. We went in at half-time down 27-26. It was the only time all season we trailed at the half.

The third quarter was back and forth with both teams trading one-point leads. I hit a couple of jumpers to keep us close and at the end of the third period, Bosse led 38-37. Bosse did a great job defending Brian as he only scored two points in the second half.

The fourth was tight throughout. We traded baskets until Scott made two clutch free throws and Tracy made a jumper to give us a 46-43 lead late in the game. I fouled out with a couple of minutes left in the game, but I was confident we would be fine. The score was 48-47 with ten seconds left in the game and Stacy was at the line for a one-and-one. Stacy missed the shot and Waddell grabbed the rebound. The key play of the game was Brian immediately guarded Waddell and slowed him down to get the last shot. Waddell could only get off a desperation half-court shot, and it was not close. We came away with a great win against a great team.

Evie Waddell was just spectacular for Bosse and finished with twenty points and eleven rebounds. Brian and Tracy scored twelve points each, I scored ten and Stacy added seven. I finished the game 5-5 from the floor in what was my best game of the year.

Coach Lee was as excited after the game as I ever saw him. He wore his green and white plaid jacket and twirled it around and he left the floor to go the locker room. It was one of the biggest regular seasons wins in the history of our school.

We never stopped to eat after games. For longer trips, we would have sack lunches that were handed out to us for the ride home. On this night, we stopped at Hardee's on the way home and Jerry Sloan bought out meals. We headed home and when we got to the Enfield four-way stop, there were several fans and police cars waiting to escort us home. It was quite a night.

*Coach Lee: After we beat Bosse, Jerry gave me $100 to feed you guys. I did not know that several of the fans were waiting for us in Enfield so they could bring us home to McLeansboro. So, I felt bad we had taken our time eating and made the fans wait for us on a cold, wintery night.*

*Martin Duffy, Member of the 1973 Ridgeway Eagles' State Title Team: The green and red crowd at Roberts Stadium the night you guys played Bosse is etched in my memories forever. For a small town like McLeansboro to fill up one side of Roberts was AMAZING!!! Coach Lee never showed much emotion. But after you won, I recall him standing on a chair and waving a green towel to the Foxes' fans. It was an awesome site. I probably saw you guys play ten games that year.*

Brian posting up against Bosse. Brian played a tremendous game against Bosse on both ends of the floor and prevented Evie Waddell from getting up a good shot at the buzzer.

Scott Cravens getting pressured by Bosse's Robert Calhoun. The Bulldogs pressured us for thirty-two minutes and helped prepare us for the post-season.

Stacy goes up for a shot against Bosse.

The program cover from the game versus Evansville Bosse. Mark Freels, Evie Waddell,
Robert Calhoun, and their teammates played a great game against us.
We pulled out a thriller by the score of 48-47.

# 37

# Game 25: Foxes 78 Eldorado Eagles 50
# Foxes 25-0

Our next game was our third matchup with the hated Eldorado Eagles. Even though we had beaten the Eagles twice, we knew we had to be ready to play. Coach Hosman's teams always competed hard and played solid, aggressive defense. Once again, any concerns of a letdown after the win over Bosse were extinguished in the first quarter.

We came out and jumped all over the Eagles. The score after the first quarter was 20-4. The second quarter Eldorado hung tough, and we led at the half 40-24. We built on our lead in the second half and ended up winning 78-50. Coach Lee cleared the bench in the fourth quarter and got everyone in the game.

We had really balanced scoring for the game as five players were in double figures. Brian led us with nineteen points, Stacy scored eighteen, Cravens had fifteen, and Tracy finished with eleven points, and Bryan Cross dropped in ten. It was pretty satisfying for us to beat the Eagles by twenty-eight points.

Brian Sloan pulling down a rebound against Eldorado. Brian dominated teams all season on the backboards and he was the difference for us in almost every game.

The 83-84 Foxes were not the only team to make it to state in 1984. The East Side Junior High Lady Foxes, led by Brian Sloan's younger sister Holly, brought home 4th place the same year.

# 38

## Game 26: Foxes 55 Ridgeway Eagles 41 Foxes 26-0

Our final road game would be against Coach Bob Dallas and his Ridgeway Eagles. Coach Dallas had been the head coach at Ridgeway for years and his teams always played a very disciplined brand of basketball. His 1972-73 team was the first from Southern Illinois to win a class A state championship. They also always seemed to have at least one really good guard and this year was no different. The Eagles were led by 5'9 Brandon Newton who was a tremendous shooter from the perimeter.

The Eagles were a pesky team and hung with us the entire game. They controlled the tempo and we never really got into the flow of the game. We led 8-6 after the first quarter and 25-20 at the half. We ended up outscoring Ridgeway in every quarter, but they hung tough. We won a tough game 55-41.

Brian led us with twenty-two points and Tracy pitched in twelve. A scary moment happened in the fourth quarter of the game when Brian rolled his ankle. Ridgeway had a nice gym, but they also had a floor that was unusual in that it was in the middle of the gym and had a lip just outside of the sidelines and endlines. Brian tried to save a ball and his ankle rolled when hit the lip of the floor. He had to be helped off the floor and did not finish the game.

Two good things came out of this game. One, we won and second, Brian was fine. He was a little sore, but he would be able to play in our last game of the season.

McLeansboro coach David Lee likes what he sees.

Coach Lee liked what he saw from our team most of the time during the 83-84 season.

# 39

# Game 27: Foxes 79 Harrisburg Bulldogs 50 (Senior Night) Foxes 27-0

The last game of the season was a rematch with the Harrisburg Bulldogs, and it was also senior night. It was an emotional night for all of us and there was no way we were going to let Harrisburg end our perfect season. Before the game, Brian, Stacy, Scott, Ernie Shelton, Heath Lasswell, and Tony Rubenacker were honored with their parents.

The crowd was the biggest all season with people almost hanging from the rafters. In addition to officiating, my dad was the girls' coach at Woodlawn High School. He brought his team over to watch the game and they sat at the top of the bleachers on the stage. I remember looking up and seeing them there and thinking how cool it was for them to come. I knew all of the players on his team and loved going to his games.

We jumped out to a big lead early and we were up 24-10 at the end of the first quarter. Harrisburg helped us out a bit as one of their players was called for a technical and their head coach, Tony Holler, picked up two himself. Bryan Cross made all six free throws and we never let up. We went into the half up 42-20. The third quarter was more of the same as we outscored Harrisburg by twelve and led 67-33 heading into the final frame.

For about the twentieth time that season, Coach Lee subbed the starters out and let Ernie, Tony, and Heath play that last quarter of the game along with the rest of the junior varsity players. Once again, Brian led us with nineteen points, Cravens had seventeen, Cross had sixteen, and Tracy finished with eleven.

When the game was over, we shook hands with the Bulldogs and prepared to head to the locker room, but then Coach Lee, once again, did something unusual. David got on the microphone and asked the fans to stay for a few minutes. Coach Lee talked about what a great season we had experienced, but that now was when we needed our fans more than ever. The Regional started the following week and one loss meant we were done.

Then, Coach Lee led the crowd in singing Eddie Allen's song *Put Another Log on the Fire* while all the players stood in the middle of the floor. At the time, I think the players thought it was kind of silly, but looking back it was another brilliant move by David to remind our fans that our season was going to get tougher.

Jeffrey Morris

# McLeansboro High School
## JIM BURNS

In recognition of outstanding athletic achievements, basketball uniform number 52 will be retired immediately following the Junior Varsity game.

Achievements By Jim

High School Basketball
A. First team All-State 1962-63.
B. Led Foxes to fourth place finish at state tournament in 1962.
C. Three years varsity starter. Teams had a combined record of 70 wins-19 defeats.
D. Averaged 24.1 points a game as a senior and 20.9 points as a junior.
E. Second leading scorer in McLeansboro history.
F. Averaged 13.4 rebounds a game as a senior and 10.5 as a junior. Second leading rebounding in Foxes history.
G. Scored 46 points in one regular season game and 85 points at "62" state tournament and made the all tournament team.

Track
Holds 180 yard low hurdle record set in 1963.

College — Northwestern University Basketball
A. All-American 1967.
B. Academic All-American 1967.
C. Big Ten First Team 1967.
D. Academic All Big Ten — Two years in a row.
E. Set school scoring record — 1368 points.
F. Captain and Most Valuable of '67 team.
E. Played in North-South and East-West All-Star games in 1967.
F. Named to Northwestern's all time basketball team.

Academic Honors:
A. Dean's List.
B. Fraternity Senior Pin Award.
C. Coyne Award (Athletics, scholarship and leadership).
D. Junior Men's Honorary (leadership).
E. Degree: June 1967 Bachelor of Arts — major history.
F. Degree June 1971: Juris Doctor — Northwestern University Law School.

Presently — Partnership in law office of Isham, Lincoln & Beale; specializing in litigation and trial work. One First National Plaza — Chicago, Illinois.

Activities — Northwestern University Board of Trustees; Vice President of N Club.

Past Experience — Assistant United States Attorney, United States Department of Justice.

Former Fox Jim Burns became the second player in MHS history to have his basketball number retired before Foxes last home game against Harrisburg.

Brian with the jumper over two Bulldog defenders. Brian was not the greatest
athlete or pure shooter, but nobody competed harder than Brian.
He was the heart and soul of our team.

Bryan Cross getting one of the few baskets he made inside of 18 feet during the season. "The Phantom" shot 70-100 for the season and about sixty-five of his made shots were from 15-18 feet.

Steve Huggins, Gene Haile (Jim and David Lee's high school coach at MHS), Jim Burns, David Lee, and MHS Principal Ernie VanZant the night #52 was retired.

# 40

# Game 28: Foxes 90 Johnston City 28 (Regional Semifinal) Foxes 28-0

This was the third game of our season in which we played almost to perfection. Ziegler-Royalton and Fairfield were the first two games and Johnston City was the third team that we absolutely destroyed.

Heading into the regional, a number of sportswriters had predicted that we would lose in the regional final at West Frankfort to the home-town Redbirds. Ironically, Johnston City had beaten the Redbirds a few weeks before we played them, and on the bus to the game Stacy and I were talking about how we need to be ready for this game and not over-look Johnston City.

We came out on fire and just got hotter as the game went on. The opening quarter we led 16-10 and we outscored the Indians 26-8 in the second period to lead 42-14 at the half. The third quarter was more of the same as we ended up leading 72-22 going into the fourth quarter. The bench players finished the game, and we ended up beating a pretty good Indian team 90-28.

Stacy Sturm had another strong game as he shot 9-10 from the field and finished with twenty-one points. Brian scored nineteen and blocked six shots, Tracy pitched in ten, and Cravens and I both finished with eight points. It was a great way to start the post-season.

Brian denies a shot by one of the Johnston City Indians. Brian protected the rim and made scoring against us inside very difficult.

Showing off my incredible 19" vertical jump and drawing a foul against Johnston City.

Stacy Sturm goes up for two in the regional opener against the Johnston City Indians. Before the game, Stacy and I talked about being ready for the Indians because they had beaten West Frankfort a few days earlier. We beat the Indians 90-28.

# 41

# Game 29: Foxes 69 West Frankfort Redbirds 43 (Regional Final) Foxes 29-0

Going into the regional final, we knew a number of people were picking us to lose. West Frankfort had a good team and we were playing them on their court. I don't think our team ever looked for motivation, but I do think we would become laser-focused when people doubted us or there might be concern for a letdown. For example, we played Eldorado three times that year and each time we won by more points and played better.

The Redbirds were coached by Tim Ricci and had one of the top juniors in Southern Illinois in 6'5 Don Peavey, who would go on to play at Eastern Illinois. They also had senior center, Danny Uhls, and a number of other really good juniors in Jerry McPhail, Doug Smith, and Trevor Weaver. Briana (Ingram) Weaver, one of our cheerleaders, probably did not know that one day she would get married to Trevor Weaver.

It was a raucous crowd at Frankfort's Max Morris gym. That gym was my favorite gym to play at in Southern Illinois. There were about 3,000 people at the game and their crowd was all over us as we warmed up. I know I was hit by a few pennies and M&Ms in the pregame warmups.

One thing we could always count on was Brian, Tracy, and Scott playing well in big games. Tracy had one the best games of his career by shooting 12-14 from the floor and finishing with twenty-six points. The game started close at first. Don Peavey was a big, strong player whose best asset was his passing. He made a couple of nice assists early and the Redbirds hung around. We led 12-8 after one period and 24-15 at the half. We blew the game open by going on a 15-0 run in the second half. We led 46-24 after three periods. Once again, the bench was cleared, and we won 67-43. We shot a blistering 61% for the game. In addition to Tracy's performance, Brian scored fifteen and Scott finished with fourteen. For the second straight year, the Foxes were regional champs.

Regional Champs!!! Even though some "experts" predicted a Redbird upset, we handled West Frankfort 67-43.

Tracy Sturm driving to the basket against Don Peavey from Frankfort. Tracy was named 1st Team All-State in 83-84. He came up huge for us on both ends during the biggest games.

# 42

# Game 30: Foxes 50 Hardin County Cougars 40 (Sectional Semi-Final) Foxes 30-0

The sectional semi-final was against the Hardin County Cougars at Duff-Kingston Gym in Eldorado. Hardin County and their coach, Glenn Oxford, came into the game with us 26-2. I don't think any of us knew much about them other than they had a great record and were going to try to slow us down. They played a lot like Ridgeway in that they were not going to take any bad shots.

This game was a struggle for thirty-two minutes. We let the Cougars control the tempo of the game and the longer they hung around, the tighter we got. The score at the end of the first quarter was 8-6 and we led at the half 23-14. The third quarter was much of the same as we out-scored Hardin County and led 35-23. Hardin County decided to play a little faster in the fourth to try to win the game and we ended up winning 50-40. At the end of the game David was furious with us because we led 50-38 and just let a Cougar player dribble in and score as the buzzer sounded. He was adamant that we never just let someone score.

The difference in the game was Brian. He led us in scoring with twenty-two points and was dominant when we needed it most. Scott and Stacy added eight and Tracy pitched in six. We did not play great, but we had to give Hardin County credit for that. They had a solid team and a good game plan.

Looking back on that game, I think if we had played a half-court trap of some type that the Cougars would have struggled with it. 1-3-1 and 1-2-2 half-court defenses are really hard to hold the ball against. But we had not played anything but man-to-man all year. The only thing that really mattered was that we won and would be having a rematch with the Cairo Pilots on Friday night at Duff-Kingston.

***Scott Cravens:*** *I'm sure in the coaches' minds, it was probably always a worry to not lose our mental focus. When you are undefeated, you can start to think about preserving your record as much as preparing for the next game. With each game, the pressure and expectation continued to get higher. We played poorly in the Sectional tournament with Hardin County. While we won by ten points, the coaches were definitely not happy with our performance. We weren't either. This was a reality check for us at this point we could not afford to have another game like that. Fortunately, we didn't.*

Brian Sloan goes up for a layup against Hardin County in the sectional semifinals at Eldorado HS. The Foxes won a tough game over Cougars 50-40.

# 43

## Game 32: Foxes 75 Cairo Pilots 55 (Sectional Finals) Foxes 31-0

For the second consecutive year, the Foxes and Pilots were playing in the sectional finals. The previous year, the Pilots were a slight favorite and got blown out by twenty-plus points by the Foxes. On this night, we were the heavy favorites. Duff-Kingston was another iconic gym that we played in. The capacity was around 3,000, but I am sure there were more with people standing in the concourse behind the upper chair seats.

This game was over quickly. Cairo tried to press us again and played a 1-2-2 in the half-court. The problem for Cairo was that they could only press after they scored, and they did not score much early. We scored the first ten points of the game, and the last basket was a lob pass from me up top to Stacy behind the zone and Stacy jumped up and passed it to the front of the rim for Brian to lay it in. Cairo called their first timeout after that.

We led 16-4 after the first period and 35-16 at the half. The second half was again more of the same as we outscored Cairo 19-13 and led going into the final period 54-27. Coach Lee started subbing and the fans were celebrating another sectional title. Brian led us with twenty-three points while Tracy had fourteen, Stacy twelve, Cravens ten and I chipped in with ten. If felt good for us to win at Eldorado simply because my having been such a big fan of the Eagles when dad was there.

We celebrated a bit and then dressed to go home. Once again, something unusual happened after the game. We were sitting on the bus waiting for the coaches to come join us to go home and the bus door opens.

The lights came on and Joe Hosman, Eldorado's head coach, steps on the bus. Joe congratulated us and then said, "Win on Tuesday, go to Champaign and bring home a title for all of us back here in Southern Illinois."

I thought it was a very classy thing for Coach Hosman to do and it solidified that this journey was bigger than just our team and our fans.

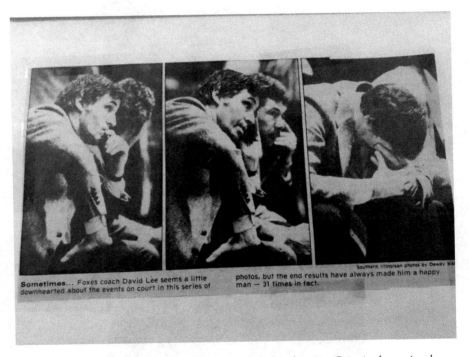

Southern Illinoisan photos by Dewey N...

Sometimes... Foxes coach David Lee seems a little downhearted about the events on court in this series of photos, but the end results have always made him a happy man — 31 times in fact.

Coach Lee and Coach Smithpeters look on as we played against Cairo in the sectional.
Going 35-0 was never easy and Coach Lee had moments of frustration with
us throughout the season.

Sectional Champs!!! Scott Cravens and Tracy Sturm showing
the sectional trophy to the Fox fans.

Stacy Sturm goes up for two against Cairo in the sectional finals.

The Foxes win the Sectional over the Cairo Pilots 75-55 at Duff-Kingston Gym in
Eldorado, IL. We were happy to win against a good team, but we were not satisfied
and knew we had more work to do in the next week against Breese Mater Dei
in the Carbondale Super-Sectional.

Scott Cravens goes after a loose ball after Stacy Sturm had caused a turnover versus Cairo. We could always depend on our defense to be solid every night.

# 44

# Game 32: Foxes 53 Breese Mater Dei Knights 51 (Super-Sectional) Foxes 32-0

From the time I was seven years old until now, I attended hundreds of High School basketball games. I saw many great games, but I always thought the best game I ever saw live was the 1980 EHT Title game between Cairo and Pinckneyville. The Panthers won 92-91 in double overtime. My dad was one of the officials and it was the most gut-wrenching game I ever watched, and I did not have a favorite team in the game. The best part of the game was my stepmom, Ann Morris, telling a Panther fan sitting next to her who kept calling dad names that he needed to shut up because that guy he was yelling at was her husband and my dad. The only thing funnier than Ann saying that was the look on the guy's face after she said it.

I now believe the 1984 Carbondale Super-Sectional against 30-0 and third-ranked Breese Mater Dei was the best game I was ever involved in as a player or coach. Mater Dei was loaded. They were a lot like Evansville Bosse in that they were smaller and quicker, but they had more offensive weapons and a great post player in Phil Boeckmann. Also, I had faced Mater Dei the year before with Woodlawn High School at the Nashville Tournament, so I knew how good these guys were.

**Coach Lee:** *I went to scout Mater Dei earlier in the season. I returned home and told Jerry Sloan and Curt Reed that Mater Dei was really good. Jerry said, "They can't be that good." I told Jerry to come with me next time. Jerry did and on the way home Jerry said, "They are really good."*

*In 1983 we beat Okawville in Carbondale Super-Sectional and in 1984 we beat Mater Dei. I had no idea how big basketball was over in that area of Southern Illinois until Darin took the job at Nashville (IL) High School in 1992. Even today, I have people over here come talk to me about the game between the Foxes and Knights.*

The Knights' head coach was Dennis Trame. I had seen Coach Trame and the Knights when he was an assistant coach at Mater Dei in 1976 when they beat Eldorado in OT at their gym. Phil Boeckmann was their best player and stood about 6'2, but played like he was 6'8 because he had about a 44" vertical. Mater Dei was a lot like us in that they played six guys. They had three terrific guards in 6' Brad Hummert, 5'11 Mark Etter, and 5'10 Ron Shadegg along with 6'4 A. J. Henken off the bench. Breese was very quick and was going to press us all over the floor for 32 minutes. Being pressed by a team like Mater Dei is tough because it not only wears on you physically but also mentally. The games against Cairo and Bosse along with the practices against the Rend Lake guys were going to help us this night. This game was an absolute 'barn burner.'

SIU Arena's capacity was 10,500 and it was sold out this night. In fact, we were told about 1000 people, including some of our fans, could not get tickets and had to listen to the game in their cars. We had a tremendous following in the "Green Wave", but Mater Dei had just as many fans as we did. The arena was essentially Kelly Green on one side and light blue on the other. It was quite a game to be a part of.

We came out hot and jumped out to an early 15-6 lead. Tracy hit a couple of jumpers and Brian was dominant inside. I think that having played at SIU Arena three times in the last two years helped us at the start of the game. In the second quarter, the Knights got their composure and the score at the half was 27-21. After the first quarter, Mater Dei just kept chipping away at our lead. The Knights continued to gain confidence and

Hummert and Boeckmann were playing really well. Brian was guarding Boeckman and I was guarding Hummert. We were all over them and they were still making shots.

**Coach Lee:** *One funny thing that happened during the game was when Coach Reed stood up to say something to one of the players and when he stood, his chair fell over. Curt did not realize that the chair had been knocked over, so when he sat down, he ended up on the floor. It was pretty funny to laugh at after we won.*

Midway through the fourth quarter, one of their leading scorers, Mark Etter, fouled out. A few minutes later, Scott Cravens fouled out trying to take a charge on Hummert. The game was in the last few minutes, and we had a two-point lead. Mater Dei was applying all kinds of pressure on us as we tried to move the ball from their end of the floor. At that time, Tracy got the ball in the middle of the floor and had Brian on his right and Cross on his left with a three-on-one break.

Every basketball team works on running a break like this in practice and our guys ran in perfectly. Tracy dribbled to the free throw line and made a perfect bounce pass to Brian. Brian caught the ball and hammered home a tremendous dunk. It was as good a dunk as I had ever seen in a High School game to that point and especially in such a big game. Our fans went berserk, but someone forgot to tell Mater Dei that the game was over.

**Holly Sloan:** *For me, the game that will always stand out in my mind was the Super-Sectional against Mater Dei. It was one of the very few close games we were in, and probably the only one I thought we had the possibility of losing. I was sitting in the front row of the baseline under our basket, and with just a little time left, Brian got the ball in his hands, and I knew it…he took a few dribbles, cupped the ball, and had a dunk that was probably the coolest thing I ever saw him do on the court.*

Mater Dei got the ball to Hummert. I picked him up high and tried to get him to give the ball up. He pulled up from about twenty-two feet and buried a jumper in my face. It was a really clutch shot by him.

With about ninety seconds left, I had the ball against their pressure and was stuck in the backcourt. I was about to call timeout when they fouled me. I went to the line and made two free throws to give us a three-point lead. Mater Dei scored again. There was about a minute left, and we went into our delay game. Mater Dei put tremendous pressure on us and finally had to foul Brian with about eighteen seconds left. Brian hit both free throws to give us a 53-50 lead. The last seconds of the game were crazy.

Mater Dei came down the floor quickly and got the ball inside to Boeckmann. Brian committed a foul and Boeckmann went to the line. Boeckmann missed the first free throw but made the second. We had the ball under their basket with about twelve seconds left. Brian took the ball out and threw it to Tracy close to the baseline in a really bad position. Mater Dei knocked the ball off Tracy's leg and regained possession.

Mater Dei did not have any timeouts, so they had to run something on the fly. Brad Hummert caught the ball on the right wing and took an 18-footer to tie the game. The shot barely grazed the rim and bounced off Bryan Cross' shoulder out of bounds. Mater Dei had one more shot with four seconds left in the game.

The ball was inbounded on the left side of the lane under their basket and Boeckmann was on the left elbow. I was guarding Hummert and when they ran their play, I saw Boeckmann was open. If I had taken a step, I could have stolen the ball, but I could not leave Hummert. Boeckmann caught the ball at about 18 feet. He took a dribble and rose up to take what looked to be an open jumper to tie the game. Right then, Brian came up and blocked the shot. The ball rolled to the half line and the buzzer sounded to end the game. We won a thriller 53-51.

The score by quarter for the game tells a lot about what happened. As can be seen below, we jumped out early to a lead and then held on for dear life for the rest of the game:

|  | 1st | 2nd | 3rd | 4th | Final |
|---|---|---|---|---|---|
| Knights | 6 | 15 | 14 | 16 | 51 |
| Foxes | 14 | 13 | 13 | 13 | 53 |

Mater Dei fell behind by nine early in the second period and then started to creep up on us for the remainder of the game. The Knights got within one point a couple of times late in the game, but they never tied us or had a lead after the first few minutes of the game.

Our crowd poured onto the floor. David ran over and hugged Brian. I remember hugging one of our cheerleaders, Julie Drone. I was ecstatic, but then I looked over at Mater Dei's bench and saw how dejected they were. I know I really felt for them. They were the best team we played all year long. It was a shame one of us had to lose. In all honesty, if Boeckmann makes that shot I am not sure we could have won in overtime.

Once again, Brian was a monster with twenty-two points. Tracy pitched in fourteen, Scott had ten, and I chipped in with six. We were now 32-0 and heading to state as the #1 team in Class A.

My dad did not get to see any of our games from the regional through the super-sectional because he was officiating. He had received his first super-sectional that year at Western Illinois in Macomb, so he was officiating the same time we were playing. Dad told Butch Williams, from Woodlawn, that he would call him to find out how we did. You have to realize that this was before cell phones, so dad had to wait a bit for Butch to get home before he could call.

Dad eventually got to a gas station on his way home and Butch answered the phone. Dad asked, "Well?"

Butch responded slowly in a very somber tone and Dad said he thought, I have missed my son's last game this year.

Butch finally blurted out, "You are going to state big boy!"

**Brian Sloan:** *I remember how big the crowd was at SIU Arena when we played Mater Dei. I had never seen that many people at one of our games. Before the game, I said something about the size of the crowd to one of the security guys and he said, "We have not had this many people in the Arena since Elvis was here in the 70s."*

**Ron Shadegg, Breese Mater Dei, Guard:** *One of the most exciting times of my life. Being able to play on that stage with such great High School players was a dream come true. Even though the outcome was not* *what we wanted, it was truly a lifelong, memorable experience. Many people in Clinton County still talk about our team and our game against you guys like it was yesterday. Thankfully, in 2015 and 2020, I was able to redeem myself by helping Mater Dei win the Carbondale Super-sectional both those years as the head coach at Mater Dei. Honestly, I was blessed to be part of one of the best basketball games in the history of Southern Illinois.*

**Mark Auten, MHS Class of 82:** *A couple of years before COVID pandemic, my son-in-law and I were going to a St. Louis Blues hockey game and had stopped at a pizza place by the parking garage. While we were eating, some guys a few tables over were talking about this great High School basketball game. They were still disappointed about losing that game. The more I listened, familiar names started popping up in the conversation like Sturm, Cross, and Sloan. At that point, I turned around and jokingly asked them if Breese Mater Dei was still sore about McLeansboro beating them. They laughed and said yes. I told them I was from McLeansboro, and we talked about the game for a while. We all agreed on one thing. That super-sectional game between Mater Dei and McLeansboro was the REAL State Championship!*

After the game, we dressed and headed to the bus. The ride home took longer than normal because there was a line of cars from Marion to the Benton exit going north to McLeansboro.

The bus ride home was great. We celebrated that win more than any other than maybe Bosse. As we approached Benton, I looked behind the bus and saw a car following closely. I looked closer and saw two heads with huge afros bobbing up and down. Now, if you have never been to McLeansboro, we don't have a lot of afros there. I looked closer, and Jimmy Tucker and Mark Auten were standing with the upper half of their bodies out of the sunroof of a car, music blaring, wearing gigantic rainbow afros. It was quite a site.

When we got to Benton, another strange thing happened. There were all these people standing on the side of the street cheering for us and high-fiving us from both sides of the bus. We finally learned the

Rangers had upset highly ranked and 27-0 Carbondale 68-58 in OT. The Ranger fans were celebrating both of our victories. It was quite a turnaround from a few weeks earlier when they were painting obscenities about us on billboards and throwing stuff at us as we warmed up.

Matt Wynn and I talked about both those games when I started this book. He felt that Benton's sectional win over Carbondale was the best game he ever saw while he was at Benton, and I said that the Mater Dei game was the best game I was a part of at MHS. How ironic that they happened at the same time.

After our season was over, Benton would go on to win the sectional and super-sectional to make it to state in AA. We were rooting hard for them to win. One, because we wanted them to bring the AA state title back to the south, but also because we could say we beat the AA champs twice.

Unfortunately, the Rangers lost a heartbreaker to the highly-ranked Evanston Wildkits. The Wildkits were coached by former Centralia Orphan and Jerry Sloan's U of E teammate, Herb Williams. Evanston's best player was future Purdue Boilermaker and Philadelphia 76er, Everette Stephens. Benton had a six-point lead late in the game but committed three straight turnovers to let the game get to OT. They lost 65-63. We all felt bad for Coach Herrin and his players.

***Mark Etter, Breese Mater Dei:*** *When I think about the game, the first thing that comes to mind was the combined records of the two teams being 61–0. That is incredible! That obviously translated into a packed arena. I'm not sure if this is accurate, but I had heard approximately 10,000 were in attendance. If that number is correct, I can't imagine that being done again. Those two statistics were the result of some seriously strong teams. I led the team in scoring and assists per game. Those facts accompanied by five points and five fouls in the game made the outcome very much more difficult. I realize that can happen, but I also remember a lot of fouls being called. That translated into too many free throws. With the quality of the two teams on the court, the referees should not let the outcome be determined at the free-throw line. Even today I'm still reminded of that game by someone in the general public. That again is* *testimony to the magnitude. Lastly, I want to say congratulations. Seems a bit late, but with the chaos on the court and my head covered up in a towel, I guess now is better than never. I'm glad the championship stayed in Southern Illinois, but wow was it difficult watching you guys at State!*

**Dennis Trame, Mater Dei Head Coach:** *We built our team in 1983-84 around pressure defense and transition offense. Early in the year, we beat Colllinsville, O'Fallon, and Belleville East, so we knew our defense would work against any opponent.*

*You guys caught our attention about midway through the season and we thought we might see you guys in the post-season. Marv Eversgerd, my assistant, and I started following your team and when we would leave games, we would hear your crowd sing "Put Another Log on the Fire." We wanted a chance to end that.*

*The excitement in Clinton County, when we were preparing for the super-sectional, was unbelievable. Fortunately, the game between the Knights and Foxes lived up to the hype. You guys had a strong lineup led by Brian Sloan and we fell behind early. Mark Etter got in foul trouble and that hurt us throughout the game. We were down 27-21 at the half but fought back and had a chance to tie the game late and that is all that I suppose we could ask for.*

*Although our players gave their all, our transition offense was just not as fluid as it had been in our previous games. I felt bad for our guys after the loss. But you all were the real deal and cruised to the state title by winning all three games in Champaign in convincing fashion. That game was, 'The 1984 State Championship Game.' That team was the most exciting team I ever coached, and it is hard to convey to younger kids how hard those guys worked and how good they were.*

**Don Hill:** *I was so lucky to start at the* Times-Leader *when I did in 1983. I had no training or experience writing for a newspaper, but I did like sports. When I applied for the job at the T-L, they gave me a stat sheet from a football game and told me to turn it into an article. So, I wrote one based on that game and they hired me the next day.*

*In the decade or so that I wrote about Foxes' basketball, I never thought much about what I wrote. After games, I would just sit down and start typing. Writing for teams like we had in the early 80s and 90s was easy. Plus, I always had guys like Sonny Aydt and Curt Reed, Sr. who were more than happy to point out my grammar and spelling errors that made it to print. That was the best job I ever had that paid almost nothing and I would have done it for free.*

Brian Sloan and I celebrate after beating Breese Mater Dei 53-51 at SIU Arena. The Foxes were heading to the state tourney after beating the Knights in the super-sectional.

Brian Sloan going up for a dunk against Mater Dei in the Carbondale Super-Sectional.

(Paul Lorenz

Brian loses the ball against Breese Mater Dei as Ron Schadegg (20) and
Brad Hummert look on.

Scott Cravens goes up for a shot while being challenged by Phil Boeckmann from Mater Dei. The Knights' Mark Etter looks on and Brian Sloan gets ready to go to the offensive boards.

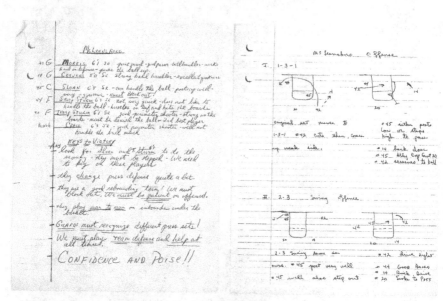

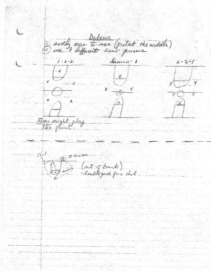

Breese Mater Dei's scouting report on us that they used to
prepare for our super-sectional matchup. I made sure to point out to Coach Lee
that they said I worked hard on defense.

# 45

# Heading to Champaign-Urbana and the Assembly Hall

One of the best parts of getting to the Illinois State Finals is the time between the super-sectional and the first game on Friday. I think all of us, especially the guys like me that did not play on the team the previous year, were feeling a sense of euphoria thinking about playing in the Assembly Hall. We knew our opponent for the first game would be the Hinckley-Big Rock Royals in the first game at noon on Friday. The rest of the matchups were:

Game 2: Lena-Winslow Panthers vs Carrolton Hawks
Game 3: Mt Pulaski Hilltoppers vs Hoopeston-E. Lynn Cornjerkers
Game 4: Flora Wolves vs Chicago (Providence St. Mel) Knights

I am confident that everyone, other than the players, coaches, and fans from the other six teams, saw the Elite Eight bracket and noticed that we were on a collision course to meet #2 St. Mel on Saturday night. It would prove to be a much more interesting tournament than most of the experts predicted.

Leading up to the tournament, we had proven to be a very consistent and balanced team. Some of you may have heard phrases like 'that team starts fast', 'their team finishes strong', or 'they are a great third-quarter team after making adjustments at the half.' I always thought playing against us was more like getting 'pecked to death by a duck.' When people ask me which one, we were, my answer is, "Yes!" We were all of those...or none of those.

After thirty-two wins and zero losses, our greatest strength was that we were so consistent. My dad once told me he loved watching us because it was like watching someone undergo surgery. We were methodical and precise and, before the other team knew it, they were down fifteen in the first quarter and had used two timeouts.

An example of how consistent we were can be seen in how many points we averaged in each quarter in the first thirty-two games of the season:

|  | 1st | 2nd | 3rd | 4th | Total |
|---|---|---|---|---|---|
| Opp. Total<br>Foxes Total | 285<br>532 | 354<br>542 | 356<br>543 | 462<br>502 | 1457<br>2119 |
| Opp. Avg.<br>Foxes Avg | 8.9<br>16.6 | 11.1<br>16.9 | 11.1<br>17.0 | 14.4<br>15.7 | 45.5<br>66.2 |

This breakdown shows that we were very consistent all year on both ends of the floor and, if I had to point out one thing, it would be that we came out and stuck people in the first quarter by holding them under nine points in the first frame. Also, heading into the Elite 8 we had won twenty of our games by fifteen plus points and only had three games decided by three points or less. Needless to say, we were a dominant team.

We practiced Wednesday like normal, or as normal as it could be, to get ready for the Royals. By this time in the year, our practices were pretty short and mostly about preparation. We were in great condition and our chemistry was in a great place. We all knew our roles and what was expected of us to help us win.

The scouting report on Hinckley-Big Rock was simple...control Jim Edmonson. The 6'6 center was averaging about 30 ppg for the season, but he had scored fifty-five in the Royals' win over Winnebago to get to state. He was a very versatile player and had signed to play at Northern Illinois. It was clear that our plan was to send two and even three people at the all-state center to force other players to beat us.

On Thursday morning we had a brief pep rally in the gym with the students and a few fans. Coach Lee reminded everyone that we still had work to do, and we needed that 'Green Wave' to help us this weekend. Our students and fans did not let us down.

Most teams who make it to Champaign take nice charter buses for the trip. One school, Carrier Mills in 1979, actually drove their players in limousines. Coach Lee did the opposite. We rode in our regular Unit #10 school bus, and I thought that it was just fine. We did not need to change anything. None of us cared. We were not kids who were pampered or needed some special treatment. We just wanted to win.

Thursday evening, we left our hotel and practiced at Champaign Centennial High School. Jerry Sloan was at practice, but he was on the floor with us which was unlike what he usually did by sitting in the top row of the bleachers. Jerry did not say much, but all of us knew that David was smart enough to ask Jerry for his input in helping us win.

Honestly, I think if Hannibal Lecter could have helped us win, Coach Lee would have told him, "Dr. Lecter, you can come to practice, just don't eat any of us."

Coach Lee told us we were going to adjust our game plan for the Royals. Essentially, he made the decision that we were not going to guard two of their players. We were playing our version of a triangle-and-two, but still staying in our man-to-man concepts. We all seemed confident that we were ready.

C & K was just one example of the support the community gave us throughout the season.

Coach Lee putting the 32nd "Log on the Fire" after the win against Breese Mater Dei.

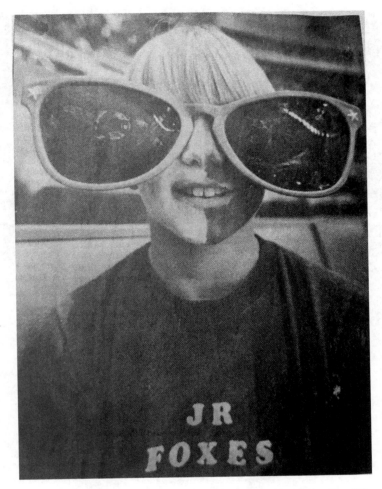

This young fan was in the midst of a full blown outbreak of "Fox Fever!!!"

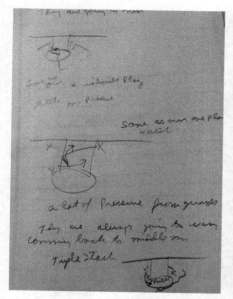

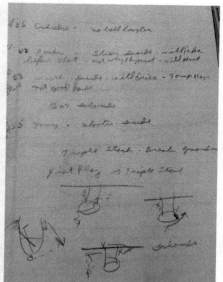

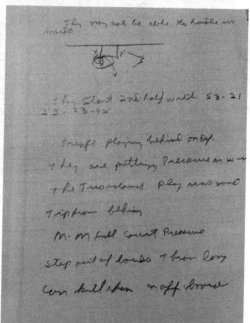

One of Coach Lee's scouting reports from a future opponent. This scouting report was for the Havana Ducks, a team we did not play, but might have faced at the state tournament. Coach was always looking ahead in 83-84 because he learned a lesson in the 82-83 season.

# 46

## Game 33: Foxes 64 Hinckley-Big Rock 35 (State Quarterfinal) Foxes 33-0

Tracy, Brian, Tony, Ernie, and Heath were on the 82-83 team that finished third, so they had done all of this before. But, Scott, Stacy, Crossy, Tim Biggerstaff, Brian Ingram, Jim Melton, and I were all new to this. Regardless, we were all excited. We left our hotel after about 11:00 a.m. and headed to the Assembly Hall. As we approached the arena, I thought of the first time I attended the state tourney ten years earlier and saw the Assembly Hall for the first time. It reminded me of the scene in the movie *Independence Day* when the humans see alien ships for the first time coming out of the fog. It was quite impressive.

Running out on that floor for the first time is an exhilarating experience. It was hard to hold it together. Now, teams are allowed to practice on the floor before they play, but in our era, the first time we stepped on the floor was on Friday when we went out to warmup before out first game.

We were ready for this game and were not going to let our season end. We came out really fast. Probably too fast for us. Coach Bob Dallas was the color commentator on the game, and he even said he thought we were playing faster than Coach Lee would have liked. I was called for a travel and Tracy threw a full-court bounce pass that went out of bounds. Tracy liked to do that once in a while just to wake Coach Lee up.

We settled down and led at the end of the first quarter 14-8. Brian was guarding Edmondson, but when he got the ball, we collapsed around him. I was barely concerned about the player I was guarding. To the point that he had the ball about 12 feet from the basket and was wide open, but still would not shoot.

Once again, we methodically worked over the Royals in the second quarter and went in the locker room leading 32-16. Things got a little interesting in the third quarter. We ran our Kansas State play to clear out Brian against Edmonson. Brian drove to the basket and Edmonson smacked the ball off the glass. The Royals missed a shot on their end, but Edmonson came over me and dunked the rebound. Then, Brian picked up his fourth foul about three minutes in the quarter.

The Royals had a little momentum. We were still up 12 and Brian was on the bench. So, we did what we did against Benton in the second game of the year. We ran our Flex offense to run time off the clock and got a shot for Crossy at the end of the quarter. And much like the game in December, the Royals thought they were playing great defense. Coach Dallas noted in the broadcast that he thought 'the Foxes are running this offense to run time and get the last shot.' He was right. We ran the clock down and led at the start of the fourth 41-28.

In the fourth quarter, we pulled away. Brian came back in and finished with thirteen points and nine boards. Brian worked his butt off guarding Edmonson. The big man for the Royals would finish with twenty-three and twelve, but he shot only 8-22 from the floor. We led big midway through the fourth and Coach Lee subbed us out. It was great to see guys like Ernie, Rube, Laz, Bigs, Jim Melton, and Brian Ingram get on the floor. I did feel bad for guys like Jim Ingram and Mark Snyder not being on the bench, because they had been with us all year and had worked as hard as anyone. But the IHSA would only let us dress twelve guys. Thankfully, that rule has been changed.

We ended up winning 64-35. The game was a bit closer than the score reflected, but it was really never in doubt. Tracy added sixteen points and ten rebounds to Brian's effort. Cravens and I added nine each, Cross had eight and Stacy finished with four. Jim Melton, Tim Biggerstaff, and Heath Laswell also got their names in the scorebook with a bucket each.

The real key to this win was on the other end of the floor. The Royals were 12-54 from the floor and shot 22.2%. If you took Edmondson out of their lineup, they shot even worse...4-32 or 12.5%. Obviously, our game plan worked pretty well. We were now 33-0 and in the semi-finals. We went to the locker room and got ready to head back to the hotel. As per our normal routine, we watched very little of the second game between Lena-Winslow and Carrolton. We left before the first quarter was over in that game to get some rest.

We went back to the hotel to eat, rest, and watch the rest of the games. The scores of the other games were:

Lena-Winslow 83 Carrolton 53
Mt Pulaski 61 Hoopeston-E. Lynn 54
St. Mel 81 Flora 48

We watched Lena-Winslow demolish Carrolton and they were impressive. They had a really good guard in 5'9 senior Justin Yeager. They also had some good overall size and ran an unusual 2-1-2 press.

The game that most people had their eyes on was St. Mel vs Flora. I knew a bit about Flora. We had played them in eighth grade when I was at East Side, and I remembered Mark Stanley being really good. They also had a freshman, Tim Locum, who would go on to play at Wisconsin. I was curious to see how they did against the #2 Knights.

We all knew about Providence St. Mel. They started five juniors and had lost in the quarterfinals the year before as sophomores fifty-four to fifty-two to Marty Simmons and the Lawrenceville Indians, who repeated as Class A champs in 1983. That game between St. Mel and Lawrenceville was memorable not only because the Indians were on a sixty-five-game winning streak (they ended up with sixty-eight straight) and defending state champs, but also because Marty Simmons, Lawrenceville's all-state center, scored all twenty-three of his team's points in the second half. In fact, Marty scored forty-three of their fifty-four that night.

St. Mel was loaded with talent. Their best player was 6'7 Lowell Hamilton, who would go on to play at Illinois with the 'Flying Illini' team that lost in the 1989 national semifinals to Michigan. They also had a great point guard in 5'7 Fernando Bunch and a good shooter in 6'2 Joe Jackson. They had depth, size, and athleticism.

St. Mel absolutely destroyed Flora. Flora was really good and had three players who went on to play Division I college basketball, but they were no match for the Knights. It was an impressive win. But we were not worried about St. Mel. We were focused on Lena-Winslow on Saturday afternoon.

One thing that I do recall about Flora was their coach, Tom Welch, was quite a character. He talked a lot to the press and after we won the state title he was quoted as saying that he still thought his team was better than us even though they lost to St. Mel by thirty-three points.

*Nicole VanZant: I'll never forget the feeling of walking in the assembly hall for the first time. I couldn't imagine I was going to be cheering in such a big place. I remember feeling a bit of fame most of that season and especially at the state tournament.*

A few students in the cheering section at Champaign.
Our students supported us all season long.

Brian goes up for a shot over Jim Edmonson of Hinkley-Big Rock in the 1984 Elite Eight. The Foxes would handle the Rocks 64-35.

Part of the "Green Wave" at the state tournament.
Our fans were a big part of our success in 1983-84.

There were actually times when our cheerleaders were a little nervous.
Nicole VanZant doing all she can to hold it together.

Running on to the floor at the Assembly Hall for the game against Hinkley-Big Rock in the Elite 8. This was a dream come true for all of us.

The Foxes move on to the semifinals after beating Hinkley-Big Rock in the Elite Eight.

Tracy Sturm takes a jump shot as I look on in our opener of the state tournament against Hinkley-Big Rock.

# 47

# Game 34: Foxes 61 Lena-Winslow Panthers 39 (State Semi-Final) Foxes 34-0

We expected to get a battle from the Panthers. They reminded me a little bit of Breese Mater Dei. Not as athletic, but they matched up well with us. There was one key to us winning this game and that was our best player and leader, Brian Sloan. I have always said that Brian came up biggest in the biggest games. Whether it was scoring thirty-two against Benton in the second game of the year or guarding guys like Sean Connor from Z-R, Bosse's Evie Waddell, and Hinckley-big Rock's Jim Edmondson, Brian played his best in the clutch. This game was about as great a performance as Brian had for us.

The game was close early. We were having a bit of difficulty with their press and solving their defense. Plus, their guards were really quick. The game was tied at the end of the first quarter 6-6.

In the second quarter, we started to open things up a bit and pounded them inside with Brian. They had two 6'5 post players, but they were no match for Brian on either end of the floor. Brian kept drawing fouls and finished the game 12-12 from the line. The score at the half was 24-17. We were in good shape so far but still had work to do.

**Coach Lee:** *I don't remember which game it happened in, but Brian was acting frustrated, and I asked him what was wrong.*
*He said, "Coach, they are doing chin-ups on my arms."*

Lena-Winslow was very scrappy and battled us as best they could in the third quarter. Both teams traded baskets and Brian continued to carry most of the load for us. We extended our lead to 36-27 after three quarters.

In the fourth quarter, the Panthers appeared to wear down and we pulled away. Our nine-point lead quickly jumped to twenty and the game was over. Coach Lee subbed in the bench players to finish the game. We outscored the Panthers 25-12 and won the game 61-39. It was a pretty impressive win considering that Lena-Winslow won the previous day by thirty.

Brian was a stud for us. He finished with twenty-six points and seventeen rebounds. Tracy and Scott both finished with ten each. We also held the Panthers to under 35% shooting from the field for the game. It was a really good win for us and now we could get some rest for the state title game later that night.

***Justin Yeager, Lena Winslow Class of 84, All-State Guard:*** *My memories of that game were that we missed a lot of good looks early in the game which allowed you guys to build and maintain the lead. In the second half, you guys ran the flex, which we were not prepared for, and it allowed you to get some easy baskets while most of our points were from jump shots because your defense kept us out of the lane. You guys also shot free throws very well the whole game which helped your cause. We all did feel that Brian Sloan got some favorable calls from the officials because of his last name, but that was just a sorry excuse for why we lost. You guys definitely played a better game and deserved to win.*

*The thing about our game I remember the most was not even about the game. It was after the game. We were all down after losing and when we were waiting on the bus to head back to the hotel, our assistant coach, Jim Cox said, "Look on the bright side, now you won't have to play St. Mel." And then Mt. Pulaski upset them. So, looking back we got our butts kicked by two State Championship teams on the same day because the following year, St. Mel had all their players back and won the title in dominating fashion.*

**Jim Kleckner, Lena Winslow Class of 84, Forward:** *Your interior defense was tough, and we needed a complete game to beat you guys. But it wasn't meant to be that night. Although you weren't the most athletic team we played, you played the best team ball and were well deserving of the state title.*

We showered and dressed to get ready to head to the hotel. Mt. Pulaski and St. Mel came out to warmup for the second semifinal, but we knew we would not watch the game. I don't think Coach Lee wanted us to be distracted by the game or fans coming up to us. However, before we left the arena I got a visit from a former Fox, Carl Mauck.

Carl came up to our team and talked to us a bit before we left. If you have never met Carl, he is a unique person. Carl was another great Foxes athlete from the 60s and went on to play in the NFL for the Houston Oilers with Earl Campbell. Carl is a pretty intense man who is about as subtle as a punch in the throat. Carl looks at me and says, "Morris, you know what I would do if I was you tonight against St. Mel? First time down the floor I would put my forearm in Hamilton's chest and knock his ass into the front row of the bleachers."

I laughed and thought, yeah, you likely would. We left before the game between the Hilltoppers and Knights tipped off.

Brian going up for two against Lena-Winslow in the
Class A State Semi-Finals.

Brian Sloan going up for a rebound among several Lena-Winslow players.
This was perhaps Brian's best game of the season. He finished with 26 points
and 17 rebounds and sent us to the state title game.

Bryan Cross getting ready to hit a jumper off a skip pass.
Crossy was clutch for us off the bench all season long.

Foxes 61 Lena-Winslow Panthers 39!!! One game left for a perfect season.

Scott Cravens locked in defending Lena-Winslow's All-State guard, Justin Yeager.
Scott was always assigned our opponents best perimeter scorer.

# 48

# Watching Mt. Pulaski Upset Heavily Favored Providence St. Mel

We got back to the hotel in time to watch most of the game between Mt. Pulaski and St. Mel. I imagine everyone, including
people from Mt. Pulaski, thought it was a foregone conclusion that St.
Mel would win. The Hilltoppers had a legendary coach in the late Ed
Butkovich, and I knew he would have them ready, but they just could
not match up with St. Mel.

I was rooming with Tracy Sturm, and we watched the game while
we rested. Surprisingly, Mt. Pulaski came out and attacked St. Mel. I was
shocked. I was sure they would try to control the tempo. But they were
hanging around and were only down 22-19 at the end of the first period.

I was thinking that there was no way the Hilltoppers could play like
this for another three quarters. Well, I was right…they played better.
For the next two quarters, Mr. Pulaski put on one of the best perime-
ters shooting displays I have ever seen. They went right at St. Mel and
showed no fear. They made eighteen and twenty-foot jumpers one after
the other. They would break St. Mel's press and just pull it on the first
open shot. It was crazy.

Mt. Pulaski led at the half 38-35 and extended their lead to 58-47
after the third. However, we all knew that St. Mel was going to make

a run. They were too talented not to get back in the game. I have to give St. Mel credit; they did not quit. They made a furious rally in the final stanza and were within striking distance with under a minute. They started fouling, but the Hilltoppers made enough free throws. St. Mel made a shot in the last few seconds, but they were out of timeouts. Mt. Pulaski had stunned St. Mel 76-74.

***Tom Shields, Providence St. Mel Head Coach:*** *Mt Pulaski did play the perfect game. Ed Butkovich was a great coach. His kids shot the lights out. After the game, in the press room, the Chicago media asked me a question about the officiating going against us. I totally disagreed. My answer was they outplayed us. They deserved to win. We did make sure in 1985 because we won the championship game by thirty-seven.*

Mt. Pulaski shot over 70% from the floor for the game and I can assure you that they did not make many layups. I am sure most of our fans thought that beating Mt. Pulaski was going to be easy. I don't know how any of my teammates felt, but my first reaction was, "This cannot happen to me with Mt. Pulaski again, can it?"

***Deron Powell, Mt. Pulaski Starting Forward:*** *We defeated Chrisman in the Super-sectional and played the first evening game against all-state guard Thad Matta and Hoopeston. They had a seven-footer but were all juniors and we beat them by about ten points. St. Mel played the game after us and I remember going up and watching them play, Coach Butkovich got us out of there after the first quarter. Pretty sure they had 5-6 dunks in that quarter and ran away with it. We were staying at the Paradise Motel in Savoy. Pretty sure that was the name, but it's gone now. It's the same place the team stayed in '76 and Coach B was very superstitious, so we were back in '84. I was rooming with our other captain, Rick Edwards. We got back to the room that night and agreed if we stayed within twenty of St. Mel that might be a win!*

*We played the game after you guys in the semi-finals on Saturday, got down 8-2 early. We made a nice comeback and led 38-35 at half. They weren't ready for the press or the fact that we would run with them. The only way to avoid getting our shots blocked! I think Lowell Hamilton only had two points in the first half and they really never tried to get it into him. We came out on fire in the second half and actually got up by fourteen at some point late third or early fourth. Our big guy fouled out, they figured out they could get easy buckets and cut the lead drastically. They were down four and made a basket with four seconds left and our guy held it out of bounds and didn't even try to pass it in. We won 76-74! We were on 'cloud nine', but knew we had another game. I remember going back to our hotel and some of our super fans bringing us Arby's to eat. It was tough to eat anything and in a couple hours we were headed back to Assembly Hall.*

After the Hilltoppers won I thought back to 1976 when my dad was at Eldorado, and they came to the state tourney as the #1 team. The Eagles were heavily favored to win the whole thing. Eldorado had Mike Duff, one of the all-time great players in the history of Illinois basketball, Barry Smith, and Eddie Lane. Eldorado was a lot like St. Mel in that they were big and athletic, and they could score. The Eagles were 31-0 and had barely been challenged all year.

Eldorado played against Mt. Pulaski and Coach Butkovitch in the Elite 8 in 1976 and they did almost the same thing to the Eagles. Led by Jeff Clements, the Hilltoppers shot lights out and upset the Eagles 76-66. I was just crushed after that loss. I have talked to a few of the former EHS players before about that loss and they said they overlooked Mt. Pulaski. They even said some of the EHS players were partying at the hotel the night before the game.

After the St. Mel loss, I looked at Tracy and said, "We cannot take these guys lightly. I have seen Coach Butkovich and the Hilltoppers do this before. If they can beat St. Mel, then they can beat us." Tracy did not say anything, but I think he knew what I said was true.

We spent the rest of the day relaxing and then we headed to have our last team meal. None of us said much about the game, but I am sure all of us knew we could not overlook Mt. Pulaski. We were focused and ready to finish this thing off. We had come too far to finish second.

**David Lee:** *At the State tournament, St. Mel was upset by Mt. Pulaski. That did not make any difference to our players. We had practiced hard and were prepared for any team. We approached each game with the same mindset and intensity.*

# 49

# *Before the State Championship Game*

Before the game, I had a small anxiety attack. I have never been very superstitious, but I did have a pair of lucky socks that I had worn all year in games. By this time in the season, these socks were more like leg warmers used in ballet. The holes in the ends were huge and the socks really served no purpose. They were falling apart, and I was not sure I could wear them. Plus, I was not able to wash them, so I washed them by hand in the sink and hung them by the heater in our room to dry. I asked Brian at dinner if I should wear them and he said, "You have to wear those things no matter what you have to do!!" I did what Brian said and that small disaster was averted.

We headed to the Assembly Hall for the title game about the time the third quarter of the third-place game between St. Mel and Lena-Winslow started. We went to the locker room to get dressed and have our last pregame with Coach Lee for the season. I sensed that Coach was a little different this time. We talked about Mt. Pulaski's players and what they did like we normally did, but David seemed confident in us. He did not say it, but I felt like he wanted us to know that if we went out and played our game, we would be state champions. He knew we were ready.

St. Mel won the third-place game 79-65. I was happy for them because I knew it had to hurt to lose to Mt. Pulaski. We were standing on the end as the teams ran off the floor and I remember that Fernando

204

Bunch from St. Mel ran off by me, gave me a high five, and said, "Win the whole thing." I thought that was pretty cool of him to do.

The Foxes and 'Toppers warmed up before the game. We had a great crowd for the game. Like I said earlier, if there was ever a time to rob a bank in McLeansboro, this was the weekend to do it. Everyone said it was like a ghost town all weekend. Stacy and I were most concerned that Coach Lee would wear his plaid jacket for the game. We were both relieved when we saw he had it on before the game.

One of my favorite memories of previous state tournaments was the television announcers for the Class A and AA games. I grew up watching Frank Bussone and Art Kimball call the games along with along with a top High School coach from Illinois. I even remembered Dekalb-Phizer Genetics being the main sponsor of the tournament.

Frank Bussone interviewed Coach Lee about our matchup with Mt. Pulaski. Frank asked how we were going to deal with Mt. Pulaski's shooters and David's response was classic. He moved closer to Frank and asked, "Have you ever tried to shoot with a hand in your face, Frank? Because we are going to try really hard to contest every shot, they take tonight." Coach Lee was kind of joking. Unlike St. Mel, we were going to challenge every shot Mt. Pulaski took in the game if we could.

One of the many trucks and cars supporting the Foxes on the way to Champaign.

# 50

## The 1984 Illinois Class A State Title Game
## Game 35: Foxes 57 Mt. Pulaski Hilltoppers 50
## Foxes 35-0 Illinois Class A State Champions

On Saturday, March 17, 1984, we played for the state title. It was ironic that our team, with team colors of green and white, won the title on St. Patrick's Day. My mom texts me every year on March 17 reminding me of that day.

We were ready for Coach Butkovich and the Hilltoppers. We knew they were a good team, but there was no way we were going to have a letdown. They had a good big man in 6'6 Rodger Cook and really solid perimeter players who could shoot from outside if left open. The game started slowly and both teams were feeling each other out a bit. Brian picked up two quick fouls in the first quarter and I am sure that David considered taking him out for a bit. He decided to trust him to play smart and left Brian in the game. The game was tied 10-10 after the first period.

We started to pull away in the second period. Brian was dominant inside. Mt. Pulaski played a lot of zone defense, and we ran a number of set plays to get shots for Bryan Cross. Coach Lee was pretty innovative in that we used a lot of 'skip passes' against zones. We would start on one side of the zone, but the whole time we were ready to have someone screen for Crossy and throw the ball about thirty feet across the floor for him to get an open jumper. Teams did not do that very much back then, but you see it all the time at every level of basketball today. We went in at the half leading 27-20.

We came out very aggressive in the third quarter and used our pressure to bother the Hilltoppers. They seemed to be getting worn down a bit and we built on our lead. Midway through the period, I somehow got a steal on three straight possessions. I had the ball out front on offense and dribbled past my defender. As I got by him, he flicked the ball from me to his teammate, who grabbed the loose ball. The kid from Mt. Pulaski attempted to throw the ball ahead for a layup, but he threw it just over my head and I stole it back. Scott Cravens hit a jumper from the elbow, and we led 32-20.

Mt. Pulaski came down the floor and ran a set on the right side of the floor for their center. I was guarding the player with the ball, and he tried to throw the ball over me to the post, but I did something that I learned at the Sloan, Lee, Reed camps years before. Rather than reach out, I put my hand up and behind my head to have time to tip the ball. I got us another steal and it led to Brian hitting a short jumper to give us a 34-20 lead.

One the next possession, a Mt. Pulaski player drove the lane from the right side and tried to hit a teammate with a bounce pass. I came up and stole the ball for a layup at the other end and a 36-20 deficit for the Hilltoppers. When I watched the tape of the game, Coach Lee stood up with his jacket off, sleeves rolled up, and pumped both fists at us after I made that layup. We scored the first nine points of the half and Mt. Pulaski called timeout with just over five minutes left in the third period. The rest of the period Mt Pulaski pressed us and sat back in a 2-3 zone. We were a little sloppy but led 40-28 after three quarters.

In the fourth quarter, we maintained a double-digit lead for most of the period. Bryan Cross hit two big jumpers and four free throws for us. The 'Phantom' had struck again by scoring ten points in the game. Cross was 3-3 from the field and 4-4 from the line. Our lead grew to 54-39 with just under two minutes to play and Coach Butkovich emptied his bench. Thankfully, Coach Lee was able to get all of our players on the floor during our final game.

Right before Coach Lee took me out of the game, I was taking the ball out on the sideline in front of our bench. Before the official handed me the ball, he congratulated me on a great season. I thanked him and patted him on the back. Coach Lee was ticked, and I could hear him behind me telling me not to do that with the official. He thought I was showing off. Fast forward to our first practice my senior year and in the first hour I made a mistake. What is the first thing David brings up? He starts yelling at me and brings up me patting the official on the back the previous March in the state title game. Coach Lee never forgot when a player did something he did not like.

Sitting on the bench we were able to relax and enjoy the final seconds of the season. Stacy and I were laughing because our crowd loved to do this thing where someone would whistle like a screaming rocket was going across the gym. After about five seconds, the student section would, in unison, yell "BOOM!" It was a lot of fun.

When the buzzer sounded, we had won 57-50 and were the 1984 Illinois Class A State Champions. We were the first team in Class A history to finish 35-0. I felt like I was living a dream. Coach Lee's reaction after we won was pretty relaxed. He just grabbed his plaid jacket and walked to shake hands with Coach Butkovich and his team. We ribbed him about him not getting more excited and he said, "You guys just made it look too easy." It was funny that he said that after how hard he had pushed us all season.

***Deron Powell, Mt. Pulaski:*** *I had never realized it was St Patty's Day until I looked up at our crowd during warmups. It was obvious they had been celebrating hardily since after the St Mel victory!! We never hit our stride and your half-court offense with Brian in the middle was tough to defend with our ball press and 1-2-2 zone. The guys we wanted to let shoot actually hit some shots and you guys earned a well-deserved victory! How could we beat a team wearing green on St Patrick's Day? Didn't seem fair right? You guys and your coaches were all very gracious. I was*

*at the IBCA All-Star game that summer and got to catch up with Brian
and Tracy…good guys."*

After the game, the teams lined up to receive their individual medals. I had watched this happen so many times with teams like Eldorado,
Nashville, Lawrenceville, and many others and we all dreamed of it hap-
pening to us. The Mt. Pulaski players received their second-place medals
and then we got our championship medals. Then they called up the
captains to grab the trophies. Brian, Tracy, and Scott received the trophy
and held it high. We all took it over to our crowd to celebrate together.
It had been a long and wonderful ride from the beginning of summer
1983, through the preseason, and winning thirty-five games to become
state champions. My first thought was how lucky I was at that moment
to be on the floor with those guys. It gives me goosebumps just to think
about it as I type.

Coach Lee, Brian, and Tracy were interviewed after the game by
Frank Bussone and Coach Dallas. They did a great job and were very
humble in how they answered. However, we did get a laugh when we
watched a tape of the game, and when Coach Dallas told Tracy he played
a great game, Tracy responded with, "Ugh…thanks, Bob."

It just struck all of us as hilarious that he would call Coach Dallas,
'Bob.'

**Brian Sloan:** *Dad had a lot of great experiences with basketball in his
life. He was one of the best players in Illinois as a senior in High School,
won a national title at Evansville, and had a long career playing and
coaching in the NBA. I am not sure where he would put that season in
terms of his time being involved in basketball, but I know he enjoyed
being able to have a couple of years at home with our family and being
able to watch Holly play at the junior high and me play at MHS. He
was never able to do that because he was playing and then coaching with
the Bulls.*

We stayed on the floor for a while after the game and took it all in.
I picked up my youngest brother, Matt, and took him out on the floor.

We talked to a number of radio stations and others around the arena. Finally, it was time to shower, dress, and go back to the hotel to celebrate.

***Pat Walsh, Mt. Pulaski sixth Man:*** *There was a reason you guys finished 35-0. You guys were super talented with great guards and a dominant big man. We definitely didn't have an answer for Brian Sloan. I just wish we could have played you on a full day's rest. After that St. Mel game, we were all gassed. We relied so much on our relentless pressure that I don't think our tanks were full for the championship game. If memory serves me correctly, we didn't have much time to rest between the St. Mel game and the title game. I'm not sure if we would have beaten you if we had been able to rest a bit, but I would have liked to have played that game with a bit more time between games. You guys were the better team though and there was a definite reason you ended up 35-0.*

*On a side note, every one of our starters and bench players on the 1984 team was successful after High School. I'm sure the same can be said about you and your team. I ended up going to SIU-C and becoming a teacher back in my hometown of Mt. Pulaski. The other memory that I wanted to share was my student teaching days in West Frankfort. I believe this would have been in 1989. Can you guess who the head coach was in West Frankfort? Yes, the one and only David Lee. I had stopped in to talk to him and let him know I was doing my student teaching there. I jokingly told him he owed me a favor after what happened in the 1984 championship game. He agreed to let me be an assistant coach and to also coach the freshmen boys' team. You talk about a great experience! West Frankfort was pretty good that year and I enjoyed being on the sidelines. I learned a lot from Coach Lee. He was one of the toughest coaches I had ever seen and understood why he knew how to win. You either busted your ass on the floor or there would be a nice spot on the bench for you. He was very intense and the most competitive coach as I had ever seen. I always admired his passion and dedication to the game. You won't find many coaches that work as hard as David Lee. I had a great experience coaching under Coach Lee. Even though I enjoyed coaching I ended up going the referee route for many reasons.*

***Dan McCue, Mt. Pulaski Reserve:*** *I don't know how many points Lowell Hamilton finished with. He had a couple of blocks, but they really didn't use him to dominate the way they could have. Our center, Roger Cook, did a decent job on him and not too bad on Mr. Sloan in the title game. Having said that, Hamilton had one dunk that was waved off for a traveling call in the first half. Then he had another later in the first half that got their crowd fired up.*

*We responded with Scott Olden, our third guard, receiving a pass against their press at about the center circle. He whipped a behind-the-back pass to Deron Powell on the baseline and Deron hit nothing but net. Took the air out of their fans and fired up ours and everybody rooting for the underdog. Scott was not a flashy player and a behind-the-back would usually have gotten us in trouble, but it was the perfect answer to the dunk. If we had made our second-half free throws, there would have been no drama, but missing a bunch of those and Roger Cook fouling out within the middle of the fourth period allowed St. Mel to come back.*

A few years ago, my son found this on YouTube. You can watch the entire game if you go to the link below:
https://www.youtube.com/watch?v=WMH2tvhBhig&t=16s.

A familiar position for me.....looking for someone to pass the ball too. I was happy to sacrifice my stats to help us win. We had too many other weapons for me to be taking bad shots.

Brian celebrating our state title. I know this was a special picture for the Sloan family because his sister, Holly (Sloan) Parrish, said "Brian was looking at Kathy (his older sister) and me when this picture was taken."

Brian Sloan comes off the floor one last time and is greeted by
Coach Lee, Ernie Shelton and Heath Lasswell.

Coach Lee offering some encouragement during the title game. Coach Lee was
tough on us, but he also knew when it was time to offer support.

The final score against Mt. Pulaski.

Getting ready to get our medals and trophy.

Scott Cravens goes up for a jumper against Mt. Pulaski in the title game.

The Champs get their trophy!!!!

The Foxes coaches, players, managers and cheerleaders celebrate a perfect season.

This layup put us up 38-22 in the 3rd period in the state final and Mt. Pulaski called timeout. During that timeout I felt like we were going to win the title for the first time all season.

# 51

## The Celebration Begins

All of us knew that there was going to be a huge party after this win, but none of us had any idea how big. We got to our hotel and there were thousands of people outside the hotel and in the lobby. We could barely get off the bus and get in to drop our stuff off in our rooms. When we stepped off the bus it was complete hysteria as everyone went nuts. For just a short period, we were like rock stars. I have to say…it was the opposite of bad. Coach Lee led the crowd in a rendition of "Put Another Log on the Fire" in the lobby of the hotel.

That night at the hotel was a lot of fun. We spent about two hours in Coach Reed's room watching the tape of the game. Darin Lee was sharing a room with Coach Reed and the VCR we used to watch tapes of the other team was in that room. Darin was in the room with Brian Sloan's cousin, whom he was dating at the time when Stacy I walked in and started watching the tape of the game. A few other players trickled in and within about ten minutes there were forty to fifty kids in the room watching the game and laughing. The look on Darin's face was priceless. We spent most of the time making fun of Brian for a play where he fell and slid across the floor like a seal jumping out of the water and sliding across an iceberg. We had to watch that play about a hundred times and we laughed harder each time.

***Don Lewis, Team Manager:*** *I remember after the championship game we were on the elevator at the hotel. Apparently, we overloaded the elevator...TWICE! The second time the alarm sounded all of us were screaming. Brian Sloan was freaking out. Coach Smithpeters and a few of us decided to not risk our lives any further and take the stairs. It was pretty funny.*

The adults were off celebrating on their own, so we just hung out in our rooms and had a great time with our teammates, the cheerleaders, and the managers. About 3:00 a.m. we went to the hotel pool and the staff was kind enough to let us swim well into the morning. We were really a pretty boring bunch of guys. I never drank in High School, and I don't know that any of the other guys did either. If any of them did, they hid it well. We all knew we had too much to lose to do something stupid and jeopardize our season.

We stayed at the pool till daylight. We were even there when the Sunday paper came in at about 6:00 a. m. The hotel manager gave us about twenty copies for us to keep. At that point, we headed back to our rooms to get ready to head home. I was excited to see my family and celebrate with them at MHS. We knew the ride home would be fun, but it was also kind of melancholy because our season was over, and we would never play as a team again. At least not against high school kids.

We loaded up and headed home from Champaign about 10:00 a.m. We had no idea the greeting we would receive at home or when we would start seeing supporters along the highway. Our bus rides were always quiet before games, and they were not much louder after. Even if we won, we never really got crazy loud on the bus. It really just wasn't who any of us were. None of us on the team were loud or obnoxious about our success. We always tried to carry ourselves with class when we represented MHS and the community.

This bus ride was different. Tracy Sturm had his 'boom box' and it blared all of the way home. Even the coaches were laughing and joking around. I think they knew we had earned this, and they seemed to enjoy seeing us be able to loosen up for one last ride home. About the time we hit Effingham, we began to see banners and people standing on overpasses waving and congratulating us on our season. Effingham is about eighty miles north of Mt Vernon and 100 miles from McLeansboro. I was shocked to see people recognizing us so far from home.

The closer we got to home, the more people we saw. When we got off the interstate at Mt Vernon, it turned into a parade. There were what seemed like thousands of people on both sides of Broadway Street waving and cheering as we passed through. It was amazing to see that many people out in a neighboring town. It was really pretty humbling, but it also was a credit to one person...Coach Lee. He was the one who set the stage with the things he did throughout the year to get not just our fans behind us, but much of Southern Illinois as well.

Once we started to head out of Mt. Vernon and reached Route 142, there were people and cars on both sides of the highway. The bus driver, Coach Lee's older brother, drove slowly to make sure we had time to wave back at everyone and let them know we appreciated them coming out. It was quite a sight to see.

We continued through Opdyke, Belle Rive, and Dahlgren. Each little town had lots of people out as we drove by. Once we got out of Dahlgren, Tracy started playing the song "Party Train" by The Gap Band. After the song finished, Coach Reed jumped up and asked Tracy to play that song again. Curt had a way about him that when he likes something, he gets this grin on his face. It is hard to describe, but we all know it when we see it. Tracy had to play that song at least four times in a row before we got to MHS.

When we hit the parking lot at the gym, we could see that the MHS gym was overflowing. And by overflowing, I mean there was no room for the 500 or so people outside to get in. We all got out and headed inside the lobby to get to the stage. Coach Reed had reminded us to think about what we were going to say when we had a chance to speak to the crowd.

Tracy and Brian led us in the gym while carrying the trophy and the game nets hanging off it. The fans parted like Moses parting the Red Sea as we came through. The scene was absolutely incredible. MHS gym held maybe 2000 people on a good night, but there had to be 5000 people in the gym, the lobby, and standing outside.

Coach Lee spoke first, thanked the fans for supporting us all year, and told them how much they helped us during the season. Coach Reed summed it up best by saying, "I don't think that being state champs has hit home with these boys yet and it likely won't for a while. But when it does, these memories will last a lifetime." Coach Reed also added that "there are 100-150 million people who could care less about us winning the state title…but they all live in China."

Most of the players thanked the fans and everyone for a great season and supporting us. Ernie Shelton did say that the fans were "the awesomest people I have ever seen."

I thought that pretty much summed how we all felt about the 'Green Wave.' Brian Sloan choked up a bit when he said, "This has been a great year. I love you all."

I do remember seeing a sea of green as I looked down from the stage and thinking about my family and how they supported me not just that year but as a young kid. The sacrifices to pay for camps and shoes and everything else to allow me to play. I also was happy to see our biggest fans, like Charlie Pendell, Dick Auten, and my grandparents, Sam, and Mona Gaines. They had been to every game, and it was great to see how happy everyone was and how proud they were.

It was a great day and a great way to end such a fairytale season. I know we were all exhausted, but none of us wanted to go home. After the ceremony was over, all the players signed autographs and took pictures. I drove my car around McLeansboro just taking it all in before finally going home for the night. Even though the season was over, and the celebration had stopped, there were still several other events that would happen that would be memorable.

March 18, 1984....the day after we won the state title we returned home to celebrate.
This was the crowd that greeted us at the MHS gym upon our return.
Coach Lee addressed the crowd with the players seated behind him.

1984 Class A State Champions!!!

Coach Lee addressing the crowd at MHS gym after we arrived back from winning the title.

Coach Reed giving one of his famous speeches at the State Championship
Celebration at the old MHS gym.

I made sure the game ball from the title game made it home safe and sound.

The Chicago Tribune had an entire page on Brian Sloan being named 1984 Mr. Basketball.

March 18, 1984, the day the Foxes returned to celebrate an unbeaten State Title season and were greeted by some 5000 people at MHS gym. This pic is from that day. You might recognize some of the people in this picture.

Bringing the trophy through a "sea of green" at MHS Gym.

"The Champs Return Home….". Brian Sloan and Tracy Sturm carry the trophy to the stage upon our return home from winning the title the day before vs. Mt. Pulaski.

# 52

# After the Season

After the season ended, I think all of us were ready to take a deep breath and relax. We had been together most days from the first of November through mid-March. After four and a half months of such an intense season, it was time to do other things. Most of us ran track in the spring and a few played baseball. However, we still had some things to do as a team.

We held our annual basketball banquet. It was a special night to celebrate such a great season along with the girls' basketball team. They had a good season as well and were on their way to building their own great program. The banquet was pretty similar to most sports banquets that I have attended, other than there were more people at ours. The thing I remember most was the guest speaker for the night…Coach Rich Herrin came and spoke to us.

I thought it was one of the classiest things I have ever experienced. Rich's team had a great year but lost two tough games to us. Then, they make the state tourney and lose a heartbreaker in the quarterfinals. The last place I would have wanted to be if I was in his shoes was at our banquet while we celebrated a state title.

Rich gave a great speech. I don't remember all of it, but I do recall him talking about the 'ABCs of Basketball' and interweaving the alphabet into talking about our team. It was quite a gesture on his part and one I will never forget. I saw Coach Herrin about ten years ago and we were talking about his brother Ron and how nice a man he was. Thankfully, I told Rich that I remembered his speech and I thanked him for doing that for our team. Rich Herrin was a great man.

We also held a couple of charity basketball games to raise money for the program. One was our team played against the Harlem Magicians and Marques Haynes. They were basically a lesser-known version of the Harlem Globetrotters. Marques and his crew came and played us at MHS. Mr. Haynes had played for the Globetrotters for years and we all knew about his ballhandling skills. At the time, I thought he was like seventy-five years old, but he was only fifty-eight when we played. That does not seem so old now that I am fifty-five myself.

The game was fun, and we played along like the Washington Generals for the Globetrotters. The Wizards were really good and even had a couple of guys who would go on to play in the NBA at some point.

We also had a father-son game. Some of the dads and a few others, like Coach Lee and Coach Reed, played a game against us. It was a fun game for all of us except Brian. Jerry and Brian went against each other, and Jerry beat Brian to death for the entire game. I don't think Brian scored a point against his dad. Brian handled it well and we laughed about it later. Away from basketball, Jerry Sloan was just a "good ol' farm boy." But when Jerry played, he was a killer. He was the most physical basketball player I have ever seen or been around. It was fun to watch him play one last time.

David also took us to SIU-C for a lunch with some of the SIU Saluki basketball supporters. At the time, I was not sure why we went, but I was happy to get out of school and hear how great we were. Now I know that Coach Lee was one of the all-time great players at SIU-C. He was on the team from 62-66 and played for one of the great coaches in college basketball history in Jack Hartman. Coach also played with a guy named Walt 'Clyde' Frazier while he was there. Coach Lee was named the outstanding athlete at SIU in 1966 over Walt and a few others. Coach Lee did say he shook a lot of hands to win that award.

Later in the spring, we were invited to a pep assembly at Ridgeway High School. Their senior class had a little extra money left over and paid for a charter bus to take us to their school. It was a really nice event. They did try to set up Coach Dallas in a banana-eating contest by having him and some other students be blindfolded and then eat a banana as fast as they could. Once the contest started, the other people were supposed to take off their blindfolds and let Coach Dallas eat all alone in the middle of the gym. Coach Dallas figured out what they were doing before he got too far and snuck a peak out to see what was going on. That actually made it funnier.

Some of the players, coaches, and managers went to one of the coal mines in the area. I did not go on that trip, but I remember being jealous of the guys who did go. I really wanted to go 100 feet below ground.

The last thing we did as a team was take a trip to the Governor's Mansion in Springfield, Illinois. We were invited to go to the Illinois Congress and then lunch with Governor Jim Thompson. The Class A and AA champs for boys and girls were invited. A few of us were excited because that meant that Chicago Simeon would be there since they won the AA title that year. I wanted to meet Ben Wilson, who was a 6'8 junior and their best player. Ben was rated as the top junior heading into our senior year in 1984-85. Ben could not make the trip, so I was disappointed. Sadly, just a few days before Simeon opened their season, Ben Wilson was shot and killed outside Simeon High School during lunch break on November 20, 1984. It was such a tragedy, and I was pretty torn up about it.

That trip to Springfield was the last time all of us were together as a team.

Some of the members of the team visited a coal mine after the season.

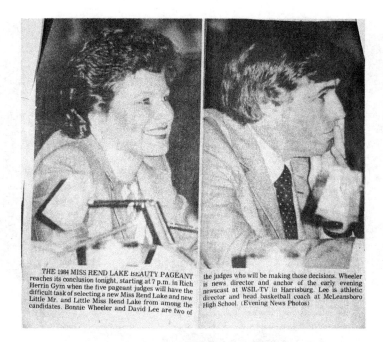

THE 1984 MISS REND LAKE BEAUTY PAGEANT reaches its conclusion tonight, starting at 7 p.m. in Rich Herrin Gym when the five pageant judges will have the difficult task of selecting a new Miss Rend Lake and new Little Mr. and Little Miss Rend Lake from among the candidates. Bonnie Wheeler and David Lee are two of the judges who will be making those decisions. Wheeler is news director and anchor of the early evening newscast at WSIL-TV in Harrisburg. Lee is athletic director and head basketball coach at McLeansboro High School. (Evening News Photos)

Coach Lee was super excited to be asked to judge the 1984 Miss Rend Lake Beauty Pageant at Rich Herrin Gym after we finished our season.

In 1985-86, five former Foxes were playing for the Rend Lake College Warriors. Myself, Tracy Sturm, Bryan Cross, Stacy Sturm and Darin Lee all played significant minutes for the Warriors in 85-86.

Lunch with Illinois Governor James Thompson after the season.

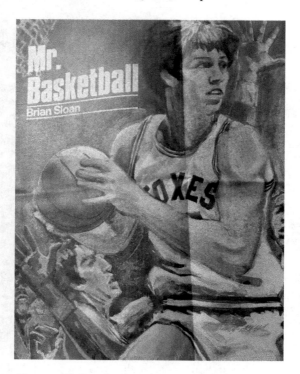

Brian Sloan is still the only player from what most consider southern
Illinois to be named Illinois Mr. Basketball.

# Sloan selected 'Mr. Basketball'

One of the many headlines announcing Brian Sloan being selected 1984 Illinois Mr. Basketball.

After the season we were invited to have pizza in Galatia and then travel to Ridgeway High School for a pep rally.

For years, people who came to McLeansboro saw one of the signs
as they entered the city limits heading in to town.

After a long season and thirty-five wins, it was time to celebrate with our families and the
Hamilton County community.

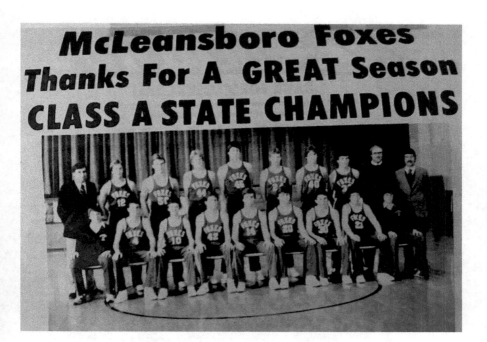

We had no idea before the season that this picture would be of the 1984
Class A State Champions.

Former Christopher Bearcat and future Illinois Illini player, TJ Wheeler,
would get autographs from players all over southern Illinois.
This is some of the autographs he got from our players.

Tracy Sturm and Scott Cravens signing autographs for some "future Foxes." After the season was over we signed hundreds of autographs for people in Hamilton County.

The watch my grandfather, Sam Gaines, bought me after the season to commemorate our State Championship season. I always keep the date on the 17th and the time at 9:45pm because we won the title on March 17, 1984 at around 9:45pm.

# 53

## *Final Thoughts on the Season*

The spring of that year was a lot of fun. I spent a lot of time with Stacy Sturm and with Brian at his house watching the NBA play-offs. Brian's mom, Bobbye, thought I was tutoring Brian in Mrs. Way's Algebra II class. The reality was that was just an excuse to hang out at the Sloan's house.

Graduation came and it was time to move on to other things. The seniors were moving on to either college or jobs. The rest of us had to get ready for next year. I spent the summer trying to get better because I knew we would have a target on our back the following season.

Once I was done playing at Rend Lake College, I lost touch with most of my teammates. I would see a few of them here and there. In early 2004, Hamilton County High School (what used to be McLeansboro High School) held a reunion for our team. Most of us made it back and it was nice to see everyone. Jerry and Bobbye Sloan were kind enough to buy each of the players a leather coat with a 1984 State Champs logo on them. I don't wear mine often, but it is one of my most cherished possessions. Bobbye Sloan was very sick with late-stage pancreatic cancer, so it was nice to visit with her before she passed away later in the spring. We went to the Sloan's new home and were able to spend time with each other one last time.

The 1983-84 basketball team was about the best group of young men I have ever been around. I never really appreciated them until the last few years. As I have gotten older, I look back and think about how lucky I was to be a part of that team. I hope that you were able to gain a little understanding of what the 1983-84 season was like.

*David Lee: As I think back on the season, I cannot pick out a favorite memory. I have a favorite memory of each player during one of those thirty-five games. Every player had a role to play, and every player played that role without complaining. Even though the last game had been played, I will always remember the reception we received when we returned to McLeansboro. Everything from being escorted from Mt. Vernon to that packed gym. That 1984 team was highly intelligent – honor roll students. Every player was always ready and prepared for every game. That kind of composure and confidence was evident in their playing of the game.*

*Scott Cravens: Just playing and completing a perfect season and having it all end in Assembly Hall. Having the championship medals and trophies presented to the players and the team. I remember the fun of winning and playing to packed gymnasiums and stadiums. The energy and excitement of the fans was amazing. Seeing and hearing an ocean of green cheering in the stands. It was an unforgettable moment.*

*The 83-84 season still comes up quite frequently in conversations with co-workers, within the community, etc. In October 2022, a manager at my job told me he was a twelve-year-old from Flora, Illinois and he was at the Assembly Hall when we won the state title. He wrote the following as part of a plant-wide distribution at Continental Tire in Mt. Vernon, Illinois:*

*In 1984, (don't judge) I found myself at Assembly Hall in Champaign watching the Illinois High School Basketball State Tournament. In the Championship game, the McLeansboro Foxes were down by two with a few seconds left in the first Quarter. At the end of the first quarter, a player took a shot from the wing, and it banked in perfectly. The score was tied 10-10 at that point the momentum began to change. Did the player mean to bank the shot? That really doesn't matter because the simple fact stands that the player stepped up and took the shot for his team. McLeansboro went on to win the state championship 57-50 over Mt. Pulaski and, more interesting, the player that made the shot to tie the game at 10-10 was the Mt. Vernon Continental Plant's Scott Cravens—he says, of course, he meant to bank the shot in because bank shots are 'cool'.*

*It's really amazing that after all this time, people still remember the details of many of the games. There were also many supporting fans from outside Hamilton County. The entire region was behind us. When you're playing basketball as a teenager, you don't realize just how much interest our winning created in the surrounding communities.*

**Brian Sloan:** *I don't really have any specific memories from the 83-84 season. What I remember is how the community supported us. I have been working at the hospital in McLeansboro for a few weeks and every day someone comes up to me just to say "hi" and talk about how much fun it was to watch our team play.*

**Don Hill:** *I always remember how good Benton was and that they had their sights set on winning the AA title that year. The games we played against them, especially the second one in the BIT, were both terrific with HUGE crowds. Games like Bosse helped prepare us for what we thought would be a matchup with St. Mel at state.*

*I also remember talking to sportswriters from other newspapers and they were impressed by our team and how quick they were. Cravens and Tracy Sturm were always great at shutting down the opponents' best guards. They also asked what I thought about Brian going to play at Indiana for Bobby Knight and how he would do there. Being able to be part of that season and that time at MHS was one of the best times of my life.*

**Bryan Cross:** *The 'big' games against Bosse and Mater Dei and at the BIT and the State Tournament are memorable for me. It was an honor to play on this team with such great teammates and Hall of Fame coaches.*

*The excitement created about the team from the fans and community was awesome.*

**Heath Lasswell:** *The first thing I think of is 35-0! An undefeated season. Not many teams have completed a season without a loss. I think of the huge crowds and the energy they brought us. We had a huge 'home-court advantage' everywhere we went. 'Put Another Log on the Fire', the cheerleaders' chants, and Brian Ingram. Brian was killed in a car wreck the following summer. I know he would have helped the '85 team.*

*After forty years, I remember things like having pizza at Auten's after games and we could not get a seat because it was so crowded. I remember the line of cars heading home after the EHT.*

*On a personal note, I remember Coach Reed staying after practice to help me work on improving my skills and get better. I also remember Brian Ingram passing me the ball at the state tournament and I scored my only basket there. We did not want to make a mistake and the look on Brian's face was priceless.*

**Ernie Shelton:** *I have such fond memories of how our school and community came together. I knew we were going to be good with a good shot of winning it all. I never really thought about winning every game until we got to state and were undefeated.*

*The Bosse and Breese Mater Dei games were both tremendous battles. Anytime we were outside the friendly confines of MHS Gym, we always had a target on our backs, but it seemed like every away game was a battle. And the fans…they were 'awesomest!' The following we had was unbelievable. Whether we were at home or in Evansville, Indiana, there was always a sea of green. Not to mention the thousands of fans from all over Southern Illinois to welcome us home with our championship trophy.*

*When that season comes up, it seems like a lot of conversation seems to be about stall ball or voodoo basketball. Our team did not stall because we had so much talent on the team, but we also had a coach who used our strengths and attacked the other team's weaknesses to our advantage. In other words, we took what the defense gave us and played extremely hard-nosed defense. For a team like Cairo who liked to play an up-tempo game, we attacked their press but also slowed it down and made them play good defense for longer than they wanted.*

**Stacy Sturm:** *The games that stand out to me from that season were the two wins over Benton, beating Mater Dei and Bosse, and also when we blew out Z-R. I also remember getting stuck on the elevator at the hotel in Champaign…thankfully, Coach Smithpeters was with us.*

*My favorite memory was coming out on the floor to warm up when the gym was packed. It was such a powerful feeling.*

**Benjamin "Benjy" Johnson, MHS Class of 1991:** *The mid-80s was a great time to grow up in McLeansboro. I was in the fifth grade when the Foxes made their undefeated run to the state championship. My memories were of large crowds and going to the games with the expectation the Foxes would win every night regardless of whether we were down ten or up twenty. I can remember going into the C & K Store to purchase Foxes' memorabilia to wear to the games and Mark Auten hauling the log into the gym so that we could 'put another log on the fire.'*

*When we made it to Champaign, I recall a nervousness as I could see the looming championship game matchup versus Providence St. Mel. When Mt. Pulaski upset St. Mel in the semi-finals, I had a sense of relief and knew there was no way Mt. Pulaski could hang with the Foxes. While I looked up to all of the players and dreamt of wearing the Fox uniform, my favorite Fox was Tracy Sturm. Tracy played for my dad at Dale, so I had an up-close view of Tracy's development at a young age. After college, Tracy returned to McLeansboro, and I had the opportunity to work out with him several times prior to my senior basketball season. He was preparing to try out for the Omaha Racers CBA team, and we spent many Saturdays playing one-on-one in the High School gym. This particular team, along with the 82-83 Foxes, not only had success but also set the stage for another generation of Foxes as they were role models for all of the kids in town and across Southern Illinois. I continue to take great pride in sharing that I'm from McLeansboro and had the opportunity to see some of the best basketball in the school's history.*

**Kelli (Ingram) Pearce, Class of 1982:** *I always think about my brother, Brian, and the overall excitement of the entire season. I never doubted that the team could win the state title. I was concerned about losing the Bosse and Mater Dei games, but winning those games was so exciting. It was not that long ago that someone brought up that season and how disciplined you guys were.*

**Craig Edwards, Class of 1985:** *The first thing I think of about this season is 'Put Another Log on the Fire' and my mom...Bernice Edwards. I started to get excited for you guys as you went into the upper twenties wins and especially when you hit the 30s. It was a magical time and it just felt like you guys were going all the way."*

*I was watching with my mom and Richard Ragsdale—my best friend of the time who usually also disdained sports but had also gotten caught up in the excitement as you guys just kept winning. As we were watching, one of the Foxes went and consulted with the Coach—then as he walked away got a swat from the Coach on the rear.*

*That prompted me to ask, "Why do they swat each other on the rear?" More probably to my mom than Richard as I assumed Richard knew as little about the customs of organized sports as I did.*

*But it was Richard who answered. He said, "Because it takes too long to kiss."*

*My Mom and I fell out of the place laughing. Your team got guys like me and Richard Ragsdale at least somewhat excited for sports events...a feat no team has accomplished since.*

**Sue Easton, MHS Cheerleading Coach:** *The overall thing I remember most is the excitement that was felt throughout McLeansboro and surrounding area. After the previous season, in which McLeansboro won third place, the goal was already set and the team, coaches, cheerleaders, and townspeople were ready for the BIG win. Support was all around.*

*The thought of losing was always there, but the support and thoughts of winning were bigger and more powerful. As the cheerleading coach I was concerned about how the team and cheerleaders would handle a loss. What could I do to support their feelings? The 'hype' was so strong, a loss would be difficult to handle. Sometimes, as adults, we forget these are young teenagers.*

*Again, the support and encouragement that was shared between the players and cheerleaders was wonderful to observe. Everyone wanted to present their best, not only in the sport but in their behavior. Being cheerleading coach for 12 years, I was fortunate to be involved in the two trips to State. I remember the looks on the player's and cheerleaders' faces when they stepped foot into the Assembly Hall and saw the floor. I still remember some of them saying "Wow, I can't believe this."*

*The ride home after winning became real as we got closer to Mc-Leansboro. A few miles out we were met by people standing along the highway with signs and cheering. This was so wonderful and really showed the kids how appreciated they were. The celebration at the gym was over the top. Another special celebration was being invited to have lunch with the Governor to celebrate the victory. This experience, especially for the kids, was one that many can say they were a part of. I remember telling the cheerleaders, once it was realized we were State bound, take it all in, enjoy this time because not many schools reach this opportunity. Make the best of it.*

*As a final thought, after reflecting on some things, this was a very special time and opportunity. I think many people really gained more respect for themselves, for others, and the community. It was truly an honor to be part of this journey.*

**Derek Harlan:** *With my mom's side of the family being from Dahlgren, I spent a lot of time in Hamilton County as a kid and consequently, went to Foxes basketball games. Despite only being nine years old, I remember that season quite well. My memories from that year include my sadness at senior night, knowing that was the last time I'd see them play at home. The super-sectional at SIU vs Mater Dei, where I was surprised to see the arena fuller for that game than for Saluki games. And the state tournament. I had never been to the Assembly Hall, and it seemed enormous. And being there seeing those final games in person was unreal.*

*Other things I remember...the Bosse game, which was televised tape-delayed on channel forty-four. We had an antenna & were able to pick it up. The patented Tracy Sturm bounce pass to Scott Cravens. Brian Sloan was always palming the ball when he picked it up or was taking it out of bounds. The set play off the opening tip of every quarter that seemed to result in a layup every single time. Being in a Target in Champaign after the Lena-Winslow game and hearing that Providence St. Mel had lost to Mt. Pulaski. Watching the bus drive by Dahlgren on the way back to McLeansboro & then following it to the reception back at the gym. Despite being so young, I remember so much of that season. You guys were so much fun to watch.*

**Becky Prince, my mother**: *My favorite memory was after you guys beat Mater Dei, all the fans ran on the floor, and you picked me up and turned me in circles. The DuQuoin game, where all the starters fouled out but you. The Bosse game was electric and also how other towns would paint signs that made all our fans angry, but just fired you guys up. I remember there was a stuffed fox in a noose hanging from the rafters at Frankfort in the regional final. I am still mad about that.*

**Steve Morris, my father:** *My two favorite memories were... First, when you guys destroyed Z-R with your pressure defense. Loved watching you guys play defense. Second, all the state tourney games. Those games were AWESOME!*

**Holly Sloan:** *I remember walking to the high school to catch the bus over to the middle school, and Tracy Sturm yelled out "Hey, Peeper!" at me, which was so embarrassing as a fourteen-year-old girl. Of course, you can't NOT hear Tracy when he hollers at you, and so I was forever dubbed Peeper by the boys on the team, and a lot of other people afterward.*

*I always loved going to the tournaments and watching the different teams walk in and sit together. You knew who they were sometimes by the way they were dressed, some wore suits. I couldn't wait to play high school basketball to be a part of something like that. I also remember that my brother would always pick me up and hug me after a big tournament win. I loved showing him off.*

*I loved all the boys on this team. They were like surrogate big brothers to me after Brian left for Indiana. I don't know if he told them to look out for me, but they were just the greatest guys. Sometimes they gave me a ride home if they saw me walking somewhere, sometimes they'd ask if I was ok if I was in my own 'drama.' They were always such great guys.*

Even after Brian left for Indiana, I spent a lot of time with Holly, Brian's younger sister. In fact, I stayed with her when Bobbye would go visit Jerry in Salt Lake City. I would stay with Holly at the Sloan's house, and we would go to my mom's house to have dinner and let Holly use our washing machine because the Sloan's was broken. Those were great times for me because Holly was like my younger sister.

On February 11, 2004, there was a reunion of the 1984 State Champions at the new Hamilton County High School. The players were presented with plaques and leather jackets to honor them for a great season twenty years later.

Coach Reed and the 92-93 Foxes finished 29-3 and made it to the sectional finals.

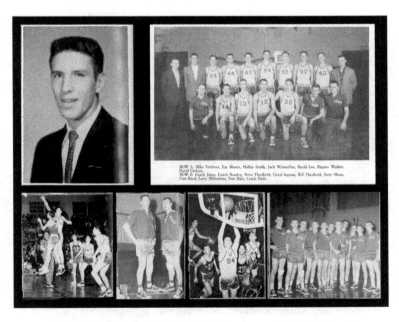

The 1959-60 Foxes were probably the best team in the history of
McLeansboro/Hamilton County High School. Jerry Sloan (54),
Curt Reed (52), and David Lee (32) were all part of this team.

*Regional and Sectional Tournament Winners*

The 1961-62 Foxes, led by Jim (52 and John (24) Burns and Tom Sturm (54 and Tracy and Stacy's dad) would finish 4th in the state in a one class system. The following year, the Foxes were even better and ranked #1 in the state, but were upset before getting back to Champaign.

The 1982-83 Foxes' team finished 31-4 and brought home the Class A 3rd Place trophy. If not for some bad luck in the Elite Eight with Darin Lee suffering a severely sprained ankle, we might have been going for back-to-back titles in 83-84.

The 1990-91 Foxes, led by Benjy Johnson, Roger "Bones" Phelps, Brian Neal, and others, finished the season 25-11 and brought home a 3rd Place Trophy from the 91 State Tourney.

Coach Reed and the 2005-06 Foxes made it to the Carbondale Super-Sectional and finished with a 22-11 record.

The Foxes basketball program had struggled a bit over the last decade, but in 2021-2022 the Foxes finished a stellar season with a 29-4 record. Coach Doug Miller and his players have done a great job bringing the Foxes back to being competitive in southern Illinois.

SITTING: Mike Webber, David Owens, Oscar Dale, Jaye Evans, Terry Whitlow, Dale Bowers, and Dennis Friedman. STANDING: Coach Wilburn Grubb, Coach Gary Burzynski, Terry Friedman, Rodney Grewe, Larry Karcher, Ken Waier, Kent Anselment, and Varsity Basketball Coach David Lee.

David Lee's first team at MHS. The 1975-76 Foxes were led by Larry Karcher, Terry Friedman, and Dale Bowers and would make it to the sectional before losing to the undefeated Eldorado Eagles.

Each of the players were given a leather jacket with a Foxes State Champs emblem at the 2004 reunion. Jerry and Bobbye Sloan bought these for these for us. Bobbye Sloan was very sick with cancer at the time of the reunion and passed away later that spring.

ow — Beverly Harl, Tracy Roberts, Kerri Grubb, Penny Wicks, Sherri Coy, Michele Lientz, Sharon Webb, Paula McNalty, Coach Willie Grubb. Front row — Beth Goodwin, Lori Clark, Chris Donelson, Frieda Rapp, Kim Hyten.

The 83-84 Lady Foxes had one of their first great teams under my kid's grandfather, head coach Willie Grubb. This team would start a run of great Lady Foxes' teams. Sophomores Lori (Smith) Kirsch, Sharon (Bowman) Webb, and Kerri (Tharp) Grubb would for the nucleus of the 86-87 team that finished 3rd in Class A in Illinois.

The old McLeansboro High School and Fox statue before the building was torn down in the 2000s. The Fox was victim to lots of "attacks" from opposing fans over the years.

The old MHS gym that the 1984 Foxes played in during the season. The "Foxes Den" was a huge homecourt advantage for the Foxes over the years.

**1984 Class A Boys Summary**

Boys - Girls | 1983 — 1985

**McLeansboro**
**State Champions**

## Box Scores of All Games
### Super-Sectionals
McLeansboro 53, Breese (Mater Dei) 51

Hinckley (H.-Big Rock) 80, Winnebago 65

Lena (L.-Winslow) 65, Monmouth (H.S.) 53

Carrollton 67, Havana 58

Mt. Pulaski 60, Chrisman 46

Hoopeston (H.-East Lynn) 51, Toluca 48 (OT)

Flora 62, Madison 52

Chicago (Providence-St. Mel) 81, Kankakee (McNamara) 51

### Quarterfinals
McLeansboro 64, Hinckley (H.-Big Rock) 35

Lena (L.-Winslow) 83, Carrollton 53

Mt. Pulaski 61, Hoopeston (H.-East Lynn) 54

Chicago (Providence-St. Mel) 81, Flora 48

### Semifinals
McLeansboro 61, Lena (L.-Winslow) 39

Mt. Pulaski 76, Chicago (Providence-St. Mel) 74

### Third Place
Chicago (Providence-St. Mel) 79, Lena (L.-Winslow) 65

### Final
McLeansboro 57, Mt. Pulaski 50

Summary of State Finalists

| | School | Coach | W–L | Enroll |
|---|---|---|---|---|
| 1 | McLeansboro | David Lee | 35-0 | 444 |
| 2 | Mt. Pulaski | Ed Butkovich | 29-3 | 225 |
| 3 | Chicago (Providence-St. Mel | Tom Shields | 30-4 | 402 |
| 4 | Lena (L.-Winslow) | Dick Laity | 27-6 | 294 |
| | Carrollton | Randy Jackson | 29-4 | 288 |
| | Flora | Tom Welch | 29-3 | 465 |
| | Hinckley (H.-Big Rock) | Gary Lane | 26-4 | 270 |
| | Hoopeston (H.-East Lynn) | Randy Feller | 26-6 | 405 |
| | Breese (Mater Dei) | Dennis Trame | 30-1 | 650 |
| | Chrisman | Roger Beals | 29-1 | 131 |
| | Havana | Scott Krause | 23-6 | 368 |
| | Kankakee (McNamara) | Jerry Krieg | 25-6 | 663 |
| | Madison | Larry Graham | 26-3 | 420 |
| | Monmouth (H.S.) | Mike Mueller | 20-9 | 550 |
| | Toluca | Chuck Rolinski | 29-1 | 133 |
| | Winnebago | Frank Lee | 25-6 | 395 |

Top Scorers

The scores and final rankings from the 1984 State Tournament.

Special edition of the Times-Leader for the 20th Reunion on February 11, 2004.

# References

Gladwell, M. (2008). *Outliers: the story of Success*. New York: Little, Brown and Company.

Wynn, M. (2020). *Rich Herrin: a head coach ahead of his time*. Words Matter Publishing.

# About the Author

Educator, Bartender, Father, First-Time Author, and lover of all things "Seinfeld"...... Jeff Morris was a starting guard on the 1983-84 McLeansboro Foxes State Title team. He currently lives in St. Louis with his dog, Griff. He enjoys spending time with his two kids, Chloe, and Quinn, who are his greatest accomplishment. He also spends a lot of time driving his golf cart all over the Soulard Neighborhood (in south city St Louis), where he has lived since 2018.

Jeff was a math teacher, basketball coach, and High School principal for almost twenty years. Since 2010, Jeff has been working in High Schools in Missouri, Illinois, Iowa and across the Midwest teaching young people how to prevent suicide.